KS2 SATs Practice Papers

10-Minute English Grammar, Punctuation & Spelling Tests for Year 6

BUMPER COLLECTION
BOOKS I & II

Ages 10-11

2020-2021 Edition

This book contains **36 bite-size 10-Minute Grammar, Punctuation and Spelling Tests** designed for **Year 6** students.

Divided into 6 groups, each one is full of **realistic practice for Paper 1 and Paper 2** of the KS2 SATs English examinations, written in line with the new testing requirements.

Each **test** is made up of **10 questions**. Each question is worth 1 mark.

Students should try to complete each test within **10 minutes**.

At the start of the book, students will find **Notes** explaining how to do the 10-minute tests.

At the end of the book, parents and teachers will find

- **Complete Answers**
- **Guidelines** for marking the **Grammar & Punctuation Tests**
- Brief, clear instructions for **Administering & Marking the Spelling Tests**
- The **Spelling Test Transcripts** which are to be read aloud to students.

Before you get started...

This book comes with FREE printable Self-Assessment Sheets & a Test Diary for students.

To access them, simply visit our website @ https://bit.ly/3gUPkPB or use the QR code below:

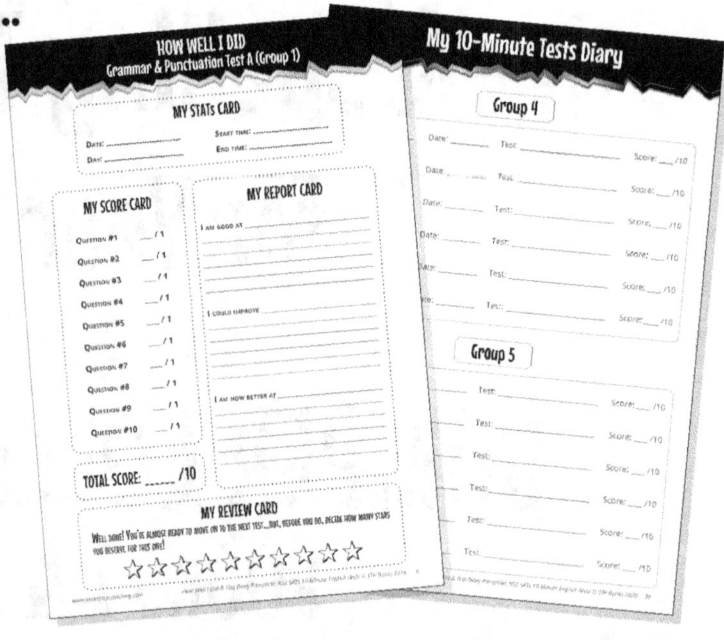

Published by STP Books
An imprint of Swot Tots Publishing Ltd
Kemp House
152-160 City Road
London EC1V 2NX

www.swottotspublishing.com

Text, design, illustrations and layout © Swot Tots Publishing Ltd
First published 2020.

Swot Tots Publishing Ltd have asserted their moral right under the Copyright, Designs and Patents Act, 1988, to be identified as the author of this work.

All rights reserved. Without limiting the rights under copyright reserved above, no part of this publication may be reproduced, stored in a retrieval system, or transmitted in any form or by any means electronic, mechanical, photocopying, printing, recording, or otherwise without either the prior permission of the publishers or a licence permitting restricted copying in the United Kingdom issued by the Copyright Licensing Agency Limited, 5th Floor, Shackleton House, Hay's Galleria, 4 Battle Bridge Lane, London SE1 2HX.

Typeset, cover design, and inside concept design by Swot Tots Publishing Ltd.

British Library Cataloguing-in-Publication Data. A catalogue record for this book is available from the British Library.

ISBN 978-1-912956-25-8

CONTENTS

CONTENTS CONT.

NOTES FOR STUDENTS

DOING THE GRAMMAR & PUNCTUATION TESTS

- Each Grammar and Punctuation Test is made up of 10 different types of questions for you to answer in different ways.
- Each question heading will make it clear to you what kind of answer is needed e.g. ticking a box, circling a word, writing a short answer.
- Each correct answer is worth 1 mark.
- You should try to complete each test within 10 MINUTES.

DOING THE SPELLING TESTS

- Each Spelling Test is made up of 10 sentences.
- In each sentence, there is a BLANK SPACE for you to fill in with the ONE WORD that is MISSING from the sentence.

- You will need to get someone to READ OUT the missing words for you from the transcripts in this book.

- You should try to complete each test within 10 MINUTES.

DON'T FORGET....

You can download your FREE printable 10-MINUTE TEST DIARY and HOW WELL I DID pamphlet for all the tests in this book from our website.

Either visit us @ http://bit.ly/3gUPkPB or, you can use the following QR code:

GOOD LUCK!

1. **Tick ONE BOX** to show which sentence should end with a **question mark**.

How to solve the problem was unclear ☐

What he'd done was terrible ☐

Who would go was undecided ☐

Where are the plates kept ☐

1 mark

2. Insert a **semi-colon** in the correct place in the following sentence.

Today's tennis match has been postponed again this is the fifth time it's been

rescheduled.

1 mark

3. **Tick ONE BOX** to show which sentence uses **capital letters** correctly.

Sandy, my Aunt Mabel's parrot, is very bad-tempered. ☐

sandy, my Aunt Mabel's parrot, is very bad-tempered. ☐

Sandy, my aunt Mabel's Parrot, is very bad-tempered. ☐

Sandy, my Aunt mabel's parrot, is very bad-tempered. ☐

1 mark

4. The **prefix** <u>re-</u> can be used with the word <u>consider</u> to make the word <u>reconsider</u>. **Tick ONE BOX** to show what the word **reconsider** means.

to think slowly ☐

to think carefully ☐

to think again ☐

to think hard ☐

1 mark

5. **Tick ONE BOX** to show which **verb form** completes the sentence below correctly.

Once Rihanna __________ up, we can leave.

is locking ☐

has locked ☐

had locked ☐

has been locking ☐

1 mark

6. Circle the correct **verb form** in each underlined pair to complete the following sentences.

The last time I had fish and chips __was / were__ when I was in Cornwall.

At the popular restaurant, there __was / were__ no empty tables.

The goldfish __was / were__ swimming in their bowl.

1 mark

7. **Tick ONE BOX** to show which option completes the sentence below correctly.

______________________________ to change for the better for a lot of people.

After 2011 conditions, in the country appeared	☐
After, 2011 conditions in the country appeared	☐
After 2011, conditions in the country appeared	☐
After 2011 conditions in the country, appeared	☐

1 mark

8. **Tick ONE BOX** to show which sentence is correctly punctuated.

Kim discovered she'd run out of sugar, milk, butter, cheese, and tea.	☐
Kim discovered she'd run out of sugar, milk, butter, cheese and tea.	☐
Kim discovered she'd run out of sugar, milk butter, cheese, and tea.	☐
Kim discovered she'd run out of sugar, milk, butter, cheese and, tea.	☐

1 mark

9. **Tick ONE BOX** to show the **word class** of the underlined word in the sentence below.

<u>As</u> she raced towards the finish line, Patricia tripped over her laces.

preposition	☐
adverb	☐
conjunction	☐
determiner	☐

1 mark

10. **Tick ONE BOX** to show the correct place for a **colon** in the following sentence.

Alice took out her red and green umbrella it was just starting to rain.

☐ ☐   ☐   ☐

1 mark

End of Test A! Now check your answers on p. 72!

1. **Tick ONE BOX** to show the **word class** of the underlined words in the sentence below.

The boys <u>were</u> hot and thirsty, so they <u>had</u> some cold water.

adjectives ☐

adverbs ☐

nouns ☐

verbs ☐

1 mark

2. **Tick ONE BOX** to show which sentence is correctly punctuated.

Lola was very confused — she couldn't understand where everyone had gone. ☐

Lola was very confused she couldn't understand — where everyone had gone. ☐

Lola was very confused she couldn't understand where — everyone had gone. ☐

Lola was very confused she couldn't — understand where everyone had gone. ☐

1 mark

3. **Tick ONE BOX** to show which sentence uses the word <u>back</u> as an **adjective**.

Gina hurt her <u>back</u> when she was playing squash. ☐

Normally, Mo gets <u>back</u> from work at five o'clock. ☐

At the cinema, Charlie likes to sit in the <u>back</u> row. ☐

We have decided to <u>back</u> the council's decision. ☐

1 mark

4. **Tick ONE BOX** to show which sentence is correctly punctuated.

The twins Annie (and Molly) are playing a card game. ☐

The twins (Annie and Molly) are playing a card game. ☐

The twins Annie and (Molly) are playing a card game. ☐

The twins (Annie and Molly are) playing a card game. ☐

1 mark

5. Complete the sentence below with an appropriate **subordinating conjunction**.

Billy will join us __________________________ he's finished eating.

1 mark

8

6. **Tick ONE BOX** to show which sentence is an **exclamation**.

He said it was the worst accident he'd ever seen ☐

When did this accident happen ☐

What an awful accident ☐

You must call me if you ever have an accident ☐

1 mark

7. **Tick ONE BOX** to show which sentence uses the word <u>left</u> as a **verb**.

In some countries, people drive on the <u>left</u>. ☐

The knight <u>left</u> the castle early the next day. ☐

Harry has fractured his <u>left</u> wrist. ☐

"Turn <u>left</u> at the next corner," Ollie instructed Finn. ☐

1 mark

8. **Tick ONE BOX** to show which sentence uses **capital letters** correctly.

He has worked at the Local Pharmacy for three years. ☐

The thief was caught by the brave Police Officer. ☐

The King of that country is said to enjoy novels by Jane Austen. ☐

I've never been inside the Houses of Parliament. ☐

1 mark

9. Insert a **pair of commas** in the correct place in the sentence below.

Selina insisted on going out despite the terrible weather to spend several

hours exploring the neighbouring fields.

1 mark

10. Replace the underlined words in the sentence below with the correct **pronouns**.

As Nora and Joyce have baked so many cakes, <u>Nora and Joyce</u> have decided to give most

of <u>the cakes</u> to friends.

1 mark

1. **Tick ONE BOX** to show which sentence is punctuated correctly.

Vera exclaimed, "It took me hours to clean up that mess"! ☐

Vera exclaimed "It took me hours to clean up that mess!" ☐

Vera exclaimed, "It took me hours to clean up that mess!" ☐

Vera exclaimed, "it took me hours to clean up that mess!" ☐

1 mark

2. **Tick ONE BOX** to show which of the following sentences is the most **formal**.

The residents have been asked to lock the gate at night. ☐

That gate is meant to be locked at night by the residents. ☐

If you are a resident, please make sure the gate is locked at night. ☐

All residents must ensure the gate is locked at night. ☐

1 mark

3. **Tick ONE BOX** to show which underlined words form a **subordinate clause**.

If you're hungry, <u>you can have some crackers and cheese</u>. ☐

The cowboy stopped what he was doing <u>when he heard the gunshot</u>. ☐

<u>Marie tidied up her room</u> before she went out. ☐

<u>After his supper</u>, Linus always has some green tea. ☐

1 mark

4. Circle the two words that are **antonyms** in the following sentence.

Initially, I thought the film was rather clumsy and boring, but, in the end, it turned out to be an intelligent, engaging piece of work.

1 mark

5. **Tick ONE BOX** in each row to show if the apostrophe is used for **possession** or **contraction**.

SENTENCE	Possession	Contraction
Let's have a party next week!		
We've got loads of homework to do.		
Diana likes shopping at the farmers' market.		
I think Jeff's shoes are very ugly.		

1 mark

6. **Tick ONE BOX** to show which sentence contains a **relative clause**.

The shirts which are in that drawer all need mending. ☐

When Carrie goes shopping, she takes her rucksack with her. ☐

I'm going to take the day off work tomorrow. ☐

The nurse said that he'd try to find the doctor for us. ☐
1 mark

7. **Tick ONE BOX** to show which sentence below is a **statement**.

Do you want to borrow a book from the library ☐

You can keep the book for two weeks ☐

Make sure you return it on time ☐

Do not spoil the book by writing in it ☐
1 mark

8. Insert **capital letters** and **full stops** in the passage below so that it is punctuated correctly.

Ravi decided to surprise his mother he went to the shops and bought lots of ingredients when he got back, he made her a wonderful stew as well as a delicious fruit salad
1 mark

9. Insert a **pair of commas** in the correct place in the following sentence.

Violet and Nina her best friend have asked their parents if they can attend a music festival in Portugal.
1 mark

10. Complete the sentences below by rewriting the verbs in boxes in the correct **tense**.

There was something wrong with the car, so I _________________ it to the garage.

> to take

Most mornings, Irene _________________ a boiled egg and toast for breakfast.

> to have

1 mark

End of Test C! Now check your answers on p. 73!

1. Write a **command** which could be the first step in the directions you give your friend to make a salad. Make sure you punctuate your answer correctly.

____

1 mark

2. In the sentence below, identify each of the clauses as either **main (M)** or **subordinate (S)**.

We put away our things after the bell rang and we left the classroom.

1 mark

3. Circle the **conjunction** in each of the following sentences.

Once Lucy had finished her drink, she threw the empty can into a bin.

I would love to go out tonight, but I am too tired.

Whenever Roger comes to visit, he always brings my mother some flowers.   1 mark

4. **Tick TWO BOXES** to show which sentences contain a **preposition**.

Polly waited for the bus. ☐

They raced to catch their train. ☐

The baby gurgled happily and smiled. ☐

Mr Harris stared at his ruined suit. ☐

1 mark

5. **Tick ONE BOX** to identify the **subject** of the following sentence.

Last May, Olivia visited her cousin in Denmark.

May ☐

Olivia ☐

cousin ☐

Denmark ☐

1 mark

6. Insert a **comma** and a **dash** in the correct places in the following sentence.

High in the misty mountains of Arkadia there lived Rune the Griffin the last
of his kind.

1 mark

7. Circle the **relative pronoun** in the following sentence.

Matthew Johnson, whose younger brother is in my class, broke his right arm
a few days ago.

1 mark

8. Rewrite the verbs in the boxes below using the **past simple tense** to complete the sentence.

Last weekend, I ______________ lunch with my friends, but I ______________ ill afterwards

| to have |

| to feel |

as I ______________ too much chocolate cake.

| to eat |

1 mark

9. Insert a **pair of brackets** in the correct place in the following sentence.

An enormous granite statue of Rameses II the famous pharaoh used to stand
in Cairo's Bab El-Hadid Square.

1 mark

10. Identify the one **prefix** which can be added to all three of the following words to make their antonyms. Write your answer in the box.

please
obey
respect

1 mark

End of Test D! Now check your answers on p. 73!

1.   Circle the two words that are **synonyms** in the following passage.

To begin with, Joseph refused to answer my question. After a few minutes though, he decided to respond with a single, grumpy word: "No."

1 mark

2.   Circle the **possessive pronoun** in the following passage.

The teacher picked up the piece of paper. After she had read it, she placed it in the plastic file which was hers.

1 mark

3.   **Tick ONE BOX** to show which **punctuation mark** should be in the place indicated by the arrow.

Millie practises the piano every morning before she goes to school she wants to become a professional musician.   ↑

comma   ☐

hyphen   ☐

question mark   ☐

full stop   ☐

1 mark

4.   Use a word formed from the root word <u>consider</u> to complete each of the sentences below.

Jamila is the most ______________________________ person I know.

I will take what you have said into ______________________________.

1 mark

5.   Use a **noun** formed from the word <u>argue</u> to complete the following sentence.

Tina lost the ______________________________ when she lost her temper.

1 mark

14

6. Insert **two hyphens** in the correct places in the following sentence.

We all thought Amir's story was terribly far fetched until we looked out of the classroom window and saw the world famous footballer standing in our playground.

1 mark

7. Rewrite the sentence below in the **active voice**. Make sure you punctuate your answer correctly.

Christopher was given an expensive present by Reem.

____

1 mark

8. Rewrite the verbs that are underlined in the following sentence so that they are in the **present progressive** form.

Mrs Singh <u>works</u> at the bank, but she <u>plans</u> to leave next month.

1 mark

9. Complete the following sentence using a **noun phrase** containing at least three words. Make sure you punctuate your answer correctly.

____ hid amongst the bushes,

watching the herd of deer grazing in the clearing.

1 mark

10. Circle the **adverb** in the following sentence.

When Penny entered the tiny room, she gasped: a large, white cat was carefully dusting a pile of old books that were on a wooden table.

1 mark

End of Test E! Now check your answers on p. 73!

1. The ________________________________ car's motor was still running.

   1 mark

2. Measles is a highly ________________________________ disease.

   1 mark

3. Ihab has always ________________________________ tea to coffee.

   1 mark

4. The weather will be ________________________________ today.

   1 mark

5. Mr Peters is the ________________________________ of our college.

   1 mark

6. Francis put the ________________________________ in his pocket.

   1 mark

7. The reckless explorer got lost in the ________________________________.

   1 mark

8. The nurse measured Riya's ________________________________.

   1 mark

9. Brian has started taking ________________________________ lessons.

   1 mark

10. *Hamlet* is a famous ________________________________ by Shakespeare.

    1 mark

End of Test! Now check your answers on p. 82!

1. Draw a line to connect each word to the correct **suffix** so that it makes an **adjective**.

Word   **Suffix**

| amuse |

| weight |

| sphere |

| ical |

| ing |

| less |

1 mark

2. Use the **conjunctions** from the box below to complete the following sentence. You may use each conjunction only once.

| but   if   or |

________________ they are good, the children can have chocolate cake ________________

strawberry trifle for dessert, ________________ not a fizzy drink.

1 mark

3. Draw a circle around the **object** in the following sentence.

Helena has written an article that is 10,000 words long.

1 mark

4. Draw a line to connect each sentence to the correct **determiner**. You may use each determiner only once.

Sentence   **Determiner**

| Is there ______ milk left? |

| No. There is ______ juice, though. |

| Okay. I'll go to ______ shop later. |

| any |

| the |

| some |

1 mark

5. **Tick ONE BOX** to identify the option that must end with a **question mark**.

Why she dislikes broccoli is a mystery ☐

Ask her why she dislikes broccoli so much ☐

Have you any idea why she dislikes broccoli ☐

She won't tell us why she dislikes broccoli ☐

1 mark

6. **Tick ONE BOX** to show which sentence uses the **colon** correctly.

You will need three: things a compass, a pen and a magnet. ☐

You will need three things: a compass, a pen and a magnet. ☐

You will need: three things, a compass, a pen and a magnet. ☐

You will need three things, a compass, a pen: and a magnet. ☐

1 mark

7. Use an appropriate **adverb** to complete the following sentence.

The old dog limped ______________________________ down the lane.

1 mark

8. **Tick TWO BOXES** to show where the missing **inverted commas** should go in the sentence below.

☐ ☐ ☐ ☐

The astronomer observed, Our universe remains a mysterious place.

1 mark

9. Put **one** comma in the correct place in the following sentence.

Racing down the street Jonah could see the bus he needed to catch.

1 mark

10. **Tick ONE BOX** in each row to show whether the sentence is in the **present progressive** or the **past progressive**.

SENTENCE	Present Progressive	Past Progressive
My brother is learning Spanish.		
He and his wife were thinking of moving to Madrid.		
Now, they are reconsidering the idea.		

1 mark

End of Test A! Now check your answers on p. 73!

1. Replace the underlined word or words in the sentences below with the correct **pronouns**.

After Rachel came in, <u>Rachel</u> turned on the lights. <u>The lights</u> flickered for a few moments and then went out.

1 mark

2. **Tick ONE BOX** to show which sentence uses the **hyphen** correctly.

In the middle of the jungle, the explorer stumbled across a well-worn-path. ☐

In the middle of the jungle, the explorer stumbled across a well-worn path. ☐

In the middle of the jungle, the explorer stumbled across a well worn-path. ☐

In the middle of the jungle, the explorer stumbled across a-well-worn-path. ☐ *1 mark*

3. **Tick ONE BOX** to identify the sentence that shows Nancy is **most likely** to be angry.

Nancy might be angry. ☐

Nancy could be angry. ☐

Nancy may be angry. ☐

Nancy will be angry. ☐ *1 mark*

4. Insert a **semi-colon** in the correct place in the following sentence.

This clock is very valuable that necklace, however, is not. *1 mark*

5. Draw a line to connect each sentence to its correct **function**. You may use each function only once.

Sentence	Function
Friends ought to be supportive, oughtn't they	statement
Friends are meant to be on your side	question
If you are really my friend, help me	exclamation
What an amazing friend you have been	command

1 mark

6.   **Tick ONE BOX** to identify the sentence which is written in **Standard English**.

The boat's sails was badly torn. ☐

Richard has done a silly mistake in his test. ☐

That jockey has ridden horses since he was five. ☐

Lucy has forgotted where she left her boots. ☐

1 mark

7.   Identify the punctuation marks on either side of the words <u>a large, grubby, bad-tempered thing</u> in the following sentence.

Toby's cat — a large, grubby, bad-tempered thing — is called 'Mr Toffee'.

____

1 mark

8.   **Tick ONE BOX** to show which sentence uses **capital letters** correctly.

My least favourite novel by Charles Dickens is *Great Expectations*. ☐

My least favourite Novel by Charles Dickens is *Great Expectations*. ☐

My least favourite novel by Charles Dickens is *Great expectations*. ☐

My Least Favourite Novel by Charles Dickens is *Great Expectations*. ☐

1 mark

9.   In the passage below, circle the word that contains an **apostrophe** for **possession**.

You can't do that now! We're extremely late. If we don't leave this minute,

we'll miss Bella's birthday party completely and she'll be very hurt and cross

with us.

1 mark

10.   In the sentence below, circle all the **prepositions**.

She stood outside the house, enjoying the feeling of the gentle rain on her

face.

1 mark

1. Using the boxes given, write the **expanded forms** of the underlined word or words in each of the following sentences.

Liam told me he <u>didn't</u> want to go out and that <u>he'd</u> rather stay at home.

I'<u>m</u> not sure I believed him.

1 mark

2. Your teacher is helping you to correct the punctuation of the sentence in the following box. **Tick TWO BOXES** to show which pieces of advice you are given.

"Who's there, yelled the guard.

There should be a question mark after the word 'guard', not a full stop. ☐

There should not be inverted commas before the word 'Who's'. ☐

There should be a question mark after the word 'there', not a comma. ☐

There should be inverted commas after the word 'yelled'. ☐

There should be inverted commas before the word 'yelled'. ☐

1 mark

3. Tick ONE BOX to show the meaning of the root <u>auto</u> in the word family below.

automatic   **auto**mobile   **auto**nomous

machine ☐

working ☐

self ☐

motion ☐

1 mark

4. Tick ONE BOX in each row to show if the use of the **comma** in the sentence is correct or incorrect.

SENTENCE	Correct	Incorrect
I don't like figs, guavas, dates, or mangoes.		
Luis who always makes me laugh, is from Argentina.		
Neither Tom, nor Hal came to school today.		
Despite the extreme heat, we all went for a walk.		

1 mark

5. Rearrange the words in the following statement to turn it into a **question**. Use the given words only. Make sure you punctuate your answer correctly.

Statement: Carl is more sensible than his brother.

Question: ____

1 mark

6. In the sentence below, circle the two words that show the **tense**.

We were stuck in a terrible traffic jam for several hours; it was incredibly boring and exceedingly frustrating.

1 mark

7. In each of the following sentences, underline the **subordinate clause**.

The knight continued to fight even though he was badly wounded.

"If you are tired," advised Mary, "have a short nap."

Wherever he went, the man found kind people to help him.

1 mark

8. Circle the **conjunction** in each of the following sentences.

"We must return to base camp," said the guide, "for it is getting late."

Once the meeting was over, we all had a lovely cup of tea.

1 mark

9. **Tick ONE BOX** in each row to show whether the clause in bold is a **main clause (M)** or a **subordinate clause (S)**.

SENTENCE	M	S
The briefcase **which is kept in the cupboard** belonged to my grandfather.		
As the queue outside the theatre was very long, **we decided not to wait**.		
The whole school will celebrate **if Sherif wins the competition**.		

1 mark

10. Circle the two **conjunctions** in the following sentence.

Cindy and Alyaa wanted to buy some new shoes for school, but the shop was closed for the weekend.

1 mark

End of Test C! Now check your answers on p. 74!

1. Add a comma to the following sentence to make it clear that **only** Ian and Ahmed started to cough.

As soon as they had left Greg Ian and Ahmed started to cough.

1 mark

2. Add **commas** to the following sentence to make it clear that **all** the children started to cough.

As soon as they had left Greg Ian and Ahmed started to cough.

1 mark

3. Use the correct **possessive pronoun** to replace the underlined word or words in each of the following sentences.

Those mittens belong to <u>the twins</u>. Those mittens are ___________________.

That bowl belongs to <u>my sister</u>. That bowl is ___________________.

Those phones are owned by <u>us</u>. Those phones are ___________________.

1 mark

4. Explain the meaning of the word **antonym**.

____

____

1 mark

5. Write one word that is the **antonym** of the word <u>miserly</u>.

____

1 mark

6. Using **adjectives** derived from the nouns in brackets, complete the following passage. One has been done for you.

The young politician was both _______**energetic**_______ [energy] and ___________________

[ambition]. At the same time, he cared for people and was always an ___________________

[attention] listener.

1 mark

7. How do the different **prefixes** change the meanings of the two following sentences?

The plumber said that the water pressure had to be <u>increased</u>.

This means that the water pressure had to be _______________________________

____

____

The plumber said that the water pressure had to be <u>decreased</u>.

This means that the water pressure had to be _______________________________

____

____

1 mark

8. Rewrite the verbs in the boxes below using the **past simple tense** to complete the sentences.

Melissa _______________ me the keys and I _______________ them to

| throw |

| use |

open the locked gate.

Freddy _______________ up and down in excitement.

| hop |

1 mark

9. **Tick ONE BOX** to show which option completes the following sentence correctly.

The mysterious man ________ bravery had saved the village quietly disappeared.

who's ☐

who ☐

whose ☐

which ☐

1 mark

10. In the following sentence, underline the **relative clause**.

The oil painting which is hanging in my room was bought by my uncle.

1 mark

End of Test D! Now check your answers on p. 74!

1. Use the word <u>set</u> as a **verb** in a sentence of your own. Do not change the word. Make sure you punctuate your sentence correctly.

____

1 mark

2. Use the word <u>set</u> as a **noun** in a sentence of your own. Do not change the word. Make sure you punctuate your sentence correctly.

____

1 mark

3. **Tick ONE BOX** in each row to show if the sentence is written in the **active voice** or the **passive voice**.

SENTENCE	Active	Passive
Jeff found a phone in the park.		
It had been left on a bench.		
Jeff took it to the local police station.		

1 mark

4. Rewrite the sentence below in the **active voice**. Make sure you punctuate your answer correctly.

The pupils were taken to the assembly hall by Mr Simon.

____

1 mark

5. Circle each of the two **adverbs** in the sentence.

When Tatiana walked into the coffee table in the dark, she bruised her knee

badly; she stubbed her toes too.

1 mark

6. Put **one** colon in the correct place in the following sentence.

The root of the problem was clear poverty.

1 mark

7. **Tick ONE BOX** to show how the underlined words in the sentence below are used.

<u>The mountain of precious jewels and gold coins</u> glinted in the candlelight.

a subordinate clause ☐

a preposition phrase ☐

a noun phrase ☐

a relative clause ☐

1 mark

8. **Tick ONE BOX** to select the verb that completes the sentence in the **subjunctive form**.

He wished the solution _______ that simple, but it wasn't.

are ☐

was ☐

is ☐

were ☐

1 mark

9. **Tick ONE BOX** to identify the function of the following sentence.

How often does this happen

exclamation ☐

question ☐

command ☐

statement ☐

1 mark

10. **Tick ONE BOX** to show which sentence uses the **present perfect** form.

Rob has been working hard and has improved as a result. ☐

Jack is trying to finish his homework before the film starts. ☐

Polly asked if she could go and see her friend, Sharon. ☐

Kelly had been asked to answer her boss's phone if it rang. ☐

1 mark

End of Test E! Now check your answers on p. 74!

1. The youth _________________________ gave a concert yesterday.

   1 mark

2. Marcus had a toasted cheese _________________________ for lunch.

   1 mark

3. The persistent lack of rain caused a _________________________.

   1 mark

4. The mayor's speech was incredibly _________________________.

   1 mark

5. Chef Pierre used _________________________ to flavour the soup.

   1 mark

6. The thirsty cow drank from the water _________________________.

   1 mark

7. The laboratory was full of _________________________ instruments.

   1 mark

8. Slowly, the plane began its gradual _________________________.

   1 mark

9. Mr Smith ran a profitable _________________________ for years.

   1 mark

10. The _________________________ of that machine is truly amazing.

    1 mark

End of Test! Now check your answers on p. 82!

1. **Tick ONE BOX** to show which sentence should end with a **question mark**.

When she comes back, I'll ask her ☐

I ought to make a call and inquire ☐

Ask Frank if he's coming tonight ☐

When is the train due to arrive ☐

1 mark

2. **Tick ONE BOX** to show which **pair of verbs** completes the sentence correctly.

After the exams, we _______ all very tired; now that we _______ rested, however, we all feel much better.

was	having	☐
were	have	☐
are	had	☐
is	has	☐

1 mark

3. **Tick ONE BOX** to show which sentence is correctly punctuated.

Carefully, picking it up the knight inspected the crystal goblet. ☐

Carefully picking it up the knight, inspected the crystal goblet. ☐

Carefully picking, it up the knight inspected the crystal goblet. ☐

Carefully picking it up, the knight inspected the crystal goblet. ☐

1 mark

4. **Tick ONE BOX** to show which sentence is in the **past tense**.

Pia is starting a new job next week. ☐

For the last six years, she has worked as a teacher. ☐

She decided to become a teacher when she was 12. ☐

For the last twelve months, she has been studying law. ☐

1 mark

5. Circle one word in each underlined pair to complete the sentences below in **Standard English**.

Rick and Tom <u>**was / were**</u> surprised to find Celia waiting for them.

She <u>**was / were**</u> standing outside their office.

1 mark

6. Draw a line to match each **prefix** to the correct word so that it makes a new word.

Prefix	Word
dis	plausible
sub	ground
re	appoint
fore	read
im	merge

1 mark

7. In the box, write the **contracted form** of the underlined words.

Mrs Fisher said that she <u>would not</u> be travelling to Belgium after all.

1 mark

8. **Tick ONE BOX** to show which sentence should end with a **question mark**.

He didn't know how much it cost, did he ☐

Ask him how much he paid for it ☐

How ridiculously expensive ☐

Don't pay more than £10 for it ☐

1 mark

9. **Tick ONE BOX** to show which sentence uses an **apostrophe** correctly.

The crowds's chants could be heard from a distance. ☐

The crowd's chants could be heard from a distance. ☐

The crowds chant's could be heard from a distance. ☐

The crowds chants' could be heard from a distance. ☐

1 mark

10. Circle all the **pronouns** in the following sentence.

She poured herself a cup of tea while Jamila and Diana cut themselves slices of cake.

1 mark

End of Test A! Now check your answers on p. 75!

1. **Tick ONE BOX** to show what the word <u>Others</u> refers to in the following passage.

Some dinosaurs, such as the Triceratops and the Stegosaurus, were herbivores. <u>Others</u>, such as the Spinosaurus and the Tyrannosaurus Rex, were carnivores.

dinosaurs ☐

Triceratops ☐

herbivores ☐

carnivores ☐

1 mark

2. Complete the following sentence with an **adjective** formed from the verb <u>imagine</u>.

That short story was the most _______________________ piece of writing I have

ever read.

1 mark

3. **Tick ONE BOX** to show which part of the sentence is a **relative clause**.

After many years, he returned to the small town where he was born.

☐   ☐   ☐   ☐

1 mark

4. **Tick ONE BOX** to show **how** the underlined words are used in the sentence.

Hugo lay in the field watching <u>the large, fluffy, marshmallow-like clouds</u> drift by.

as a preposition phrase ☐

as a main clause ☐

as a noun phrase ☐

as a relative clause ☐

1 mark

5. Name the **punctuation mark** used between the two main clauses in the sentence below.

The stone statue, which stands in the middle of the square, is over five hundred years old: many tourists come to see it during the summer months — especially August.

____

1 mark

6. **Tick ONE BOX** in each row to show how the **modal verb** affects the meaning of each sentence.

SENTENCE	Certainty	Possibility
We might take the day off tomorrow.		
It could be that we are not alone in the universe.		
Bahaa can do difficult sums in his head.		
Vince may have an answer to your question.		

1 mark

7. **Tick ONE BOX** in each row to show whether the clause in bold is a **main clause (M)** or a **subordinate clause (S)**.

SENTENCE	M	S
When Gordon arrived at the station, **he checked the time**.		
His watch, **which had been a present from his uncle**, told him it was midday.		
Gordon was relieved, for **he'd been worried that he'd be late**.		

1 mark

8. Circle **ALL** the **conjunctions** in the following sentences.

Last Thursday, Wendy was in a very good mood because she had just received some great news.

Amira, her oldest friend, was planning to move back to Manchester after she had finished her university degree.

Although they had been friends since childhood, they hadn't lived in the same city for years.

1 mark

9. Circle the two words in the following sentence that are **antonyms**.

Eating nutritious food will not entirely prevent you from becoming ill, but it will increase your chances of staying healthy.

1 mark

10. **Tick ALL** the sentences that contain a **preposition**.

While he knew he was right, Ali didn't contradict her. ☐

Recently, food prices have gone up. ☐

A small frog hopped onto the large lily pad. ☐

The results will be announced towards midday. ☐

1 mark

End of Test B! Now check your answers on p. 75!

1. Use the word <u>object</u> as a **verb** in a sentence of your own. Do not change the word. Make sure you punctuate your sentence correctly.

____

1 mark

2. Use the word <u>object</u> as a **noun** in a sentence of your own. Do not change the word. Make sure you punctuate your sentence correctly.

____

1 mark

3. **Tick ONE BOX** to show the meaning of the root <u>therm</u> in the word family below.

thermal　　**thermometer**　　**thermostat**

measurement ☐

heat ☐

health ☐

material ☐

1 mark

4. Draw a line to match each word to its correct **antonym**.

Word	**Antonym**
protest	darken
release	transparent
illuminate	accept
opaque	capture

1 mark

5. Rewrite the following sentence, adding a **subordinate clause**. Remember to punctuate your sentence correctly.

The pirate grinned at his captives.

____

1 mark

6. Label the boxes below with **V (verb)**, **S (subject)** and **O (object)** to show the parts of the sentence.

<u>Felicity</u> <u>watered</u> <u>the plants</u>.

☐ ☐ ☐

1 mark

7. Circle all the words in the sentences below that should start with a **capital letter**.

abraham   lincoln   was   the   sixteenth   president   of   the   united   states.   he   was

assassinated   in   april,   1865.

1 mark

8. **Tick ONE BOX** to show which sentence is written in the **active voice**.

Our luggage was sent to India by mistake. ☐

Pens, pencils and paper have been provided for the students. ☐

The crate had been emptied. ☐

The news had resulted in a great deal of celebration. ☐

1 mark

9. **Tick ONE BOX** to show which sentence is punctuated correctly.

The goblins — long the enemies of the elves joined forces with the wizard. ☐

The goblins — long the enemies — of the elves joined forces with the wizard. ☐

The goblins — long the enemies of the elves — joined forces with the wizard. ☐

The goblins — long the enemies of the elves joined forces — with the wizard. ☐

1 mark

10. **Tick ONE BOX** to show the correct place for a **dash** in the sentence below.

The storm had caused utter devastation everything was completely ruined.

☐ ☐ ☐ ☐

1 mark

End of Test C! Now check your answers on p. 75!

1.   **Tick ONE BOX** to show which sentence below uses the **past progressive**.

Ivan went to the bookshop to buy Maggie a present. ☐

Greg has been reading that novel for two months now. ☐

After she'd finished her book, Sue put it back on the shelf. ☐

Rania was reading the newspaper when her phone rang. ☐

1 mark

2.   **Tick ONE BOX** to show which sentence below is a **command**.

When this programme is over, you will have to go to bed. ☐

Once you've finished using the hoover, put it back in the cupboard. ☐

The general ordered the soldiers to fire their guns. ☐

The instructions are written on the back of the box. ☐

1 mark

3.   Rewrite the following statement as **direct speech**. Remember to punctuate your answer correctly.

He told her that he would look after the children.

He told her, ____

____

1 mark

4.   Insert a pair of **brackets** in the correct place in the following sentence.

Ava whose maternal grandparents live in a small town in the north of Canada

wants to improve her French.

1 mark

5.   **Tick ONE BOX** in each row to show if the underlined word is an **adjective** or an **adverb**.

SENTENCE	Adjective	Adverb
Murphy walked into the <u>wrong</u> room.		
Keith worked <u>hard</u> all the time.		
I had a <u>quick</u> lunch.		
He looked <u>straight</u> at me.		

1 mark

6.   Complete the following sentence with an **adverb** formed from the adjective <u>happy</u>.

When asked to help out at their local charity shop last weekend, Molly and Amit

__________________________________ agreed.   1 mark

7.   **Tick ONE BOX** to show which sentence below uses the **hyphen** correctly.

A sixty-five year-old woman has broken the world record.   ☐

A sixty-five-year old woman has broken the world record.   ☐

A sixty-five-year-old-woman has broken the world record.   ☐

A sixty-five-year-old woman has broken the world record.   ☐   1 mark

8.   Rewrite the following sentence in the **passive voice**. Punctuate your sentence correctly.

The activist hurled a brick through the window.

____   1 mark

9.   **Tick ONE BOX** in each row to show whether the word <u>before</u> is being used as a **preposition** or as a **subordinating conjunction**.

SENTENCE	Preposition	Subordinating conjunction
The choice <u>before</u> them was a difficult one.		
<u>Before</u> you go, please take out the rubbish.		
<u>Before</u> the autumn, we will have to do this.		

1 mark

10.   Complete the following sentence so that it uses the **subjunctive form**.

She suggested that he ______________ another job.   1 mark

End of Test D! Now check your answers on p. 75!

1. Complete the following table by adding a **suffix** to each noun to make an **adjective**.

Noun	Adjective
hair	
dot	
plenty	
horizon	

1 mark

2. **Tick ONE BOX** in each row to show whether the word in bold is a **subordinating conjunction** or a **co-ordinating conjunction**.

SENTENCE	Subordinating conjunction	Co-ordinating conjunction
Although it was sunny, Pam stayed at home.		
He turned on the fan, **for** it was hot.		
The sun shone **and** all was right with the world.		

1 mark

3. Circle all the **determiners** in the following sentence.

The   picture   on   that   wall   is   mine;   I   drew   it   two   years   ago.

1 mark

4. Write a sentence that lists all the information given in the following box. Remember to punctuate your answer correctly.

Things you need to make hot porridge
oats
milk
yoghurt
honey
brown sugar

____

____

____

1 mark

5. Underline the longest possible **noun phrase** in the following sentence.

Martin's story about his holiday was unbelievable.

1 mark

6. Underline the **verb form** in the **present perfect** in the following passage.

As she enjoys travelling immensely, Phoebe has been to many places all over the world. Last year, she visited Singapore which lies one degree north of the equator.

1 mark

7. Complete the following sentence with a **possessive pronoun**.

Those Rollerblades belong to them; they are _______________.

1 mark

8. Circle the **adverb** in the following sentence.

Malik often wondered if his life would have been different if he'd stayed in his hometown.

1 mark

9. Insert a **colon** in the correct place in the following sentence.

These expensive designer shoes come in three colours light blue, emerald green and jet black.

1 mark

10. Tick ONE BOX to show which **punctuation mark** should be in the place indicated by the arrow.

Jemma often travels to Edinburgh at the weekends since her parents have lived there for quite a while twenty years to be exact.

hyphen	☐
question mark	☐
bracket	☐
dash	☐

1 mark

End of Test E! Now check your answers on p. 76!

1. The ___________________________ rumour was started by Joel.

   1 mark

2. Helen addressed the small ___________________________ carefully.

   1 mark

3. Kristin looked ___________________________, but she didn't argue.

   1 mark

4. Our netball ___________________________ is always at four o'clock.

   1 mark

5. An adverb can sometimes ___________________________ a verb.

   1 mark

6. Britain made an uneasy ___________________________ with France.

   1 mark

7. Feeding the cat was John's only ___________________________.

   1 mark

8. Penny's knowledge of geography is ___________________________.

   1 mark

9. An owl was perched on the tree's topmost ___________________________.

   1 mark

10. Mike has always wanted to play the ___________________________.

    1 mark

End of Test! Now check your answers on p. 83!

1. **Tick ONE BOX** to show which sentence should end with an **exclamation mark**.

Wash in cold water before wearing for the first time ☐

The women all looked very glamorous in their evening dresses ☐

How pretty she looked in that gown ☐

Did you see Jasper in his dinner jacket ☐

1 mark

2. Insert a **dash** in the correct place in the following sentence.

There   is   only   one   solution   to   the   problem   work.

1 mark

3. **Tick ONE BOX** to show which sentence uses **capital letters** correctly.

Last Tuesday, at the theatre, we saw a shakespeare Play: *Hamlet.* ☐

Last Tuesday, at the theatre, we saw a Shakespeare play: *Hamlet.* ☐

Last tuesday, at the theatre, we saw a Shakespeare play: *Hamlet.* ☐

last Tuesday, at the theatre, we saw a Shakespeare play: *Hamlet.* ☐

1 mark

4. The **prefix bi-** can be used with the word <u>annual</u> to make the word <u>biannual</u>. **Tick ONE BOX** to show what the word **biannual** means.

every year ☐

every two years ☐

twice every other year ☐

twice a year ☐

1 mark

5. **Tick ONE BOX** to show which **verb form** completes the sentence below correctly.

The bookshelves are much tidier now that Maria _______ them.

had organised ☐

has organised ☐

was organised ☐

are organising ☐

1 mark

6.   Circle the correct **verb form** in each underlined pair to complete the following sentences.

It **don't / doesn't** feel very warm today.

Sue and Francis **don't / doesn't** believe in ghosts.

Nolan argued that we **don't / doesn't** need to keep buying lots of unnecessary things.   *1 mark*

7.   **Tick ONE BOX** to show which option completes the sentence below correctly.

______________________________ to warn them of the danger.

As fast as possible, Raymond raced ☐

As fast as possible Raymond raced, ☐

As fast as possible Raymond, raced ☐

As fast as, possible Raymond raced ☐   *1 mark*

8.   **Tick ONE BOX** to show which sentence is correctly punctuated.

I want to read a book, watch TV, listen to music, and go swimming at the same time. ☐

I want to read a book, watch TV, listen to music and, go swimming at the same time. ☐

I want to read a book, watch TV listen to music and go swimming at the same time. ☐

I want to read a book, watch TV, listen to music and go swimming at the same time. ☐   *1 mark*

9.   **Tick ONE BOX** to show the **word class** of the underlined word in the sentence below.

You'd better hurry up and eat that ice cream <u>before</u> it melts!

conjunction ☐

adverb ☐

preposition ☐

adjective ☐   *1 mark*

10.   **Tick ONE BOX** to show the correct place for a **semi-colon** in the following sentence.

The doorbell rang we all looked at each other in great surprise.

☐ ☐   ☐   ☐   *1 mark*

End of Test A! Now check your answers on p. 76!

1. **Tick ONE BOX** to show the **word class** of the underlined words in the sentence below.

The girl who <u>is</u> standing by the gates <u>has</u> <u>been</u> elected to the student council.

adverbs ☐

nouns ☐

verbs ☐

adjectives ☐

1 mark

2. **Tick ONE BOX** to show which sentence is correctly punctuated.

I like the idea of: a hybrid a car that uses both petrol and electricity. ☐

I like the idea of a hybrid: a car that uses both petrol and electricity. ☐

I like the idea of a hybrid a car that uses: both petrol and electricity. ☐

I like the idea of a hybrid a car that uses both: petrol and electricity. ☐

1 mark

3. **Tick ONE BOX** to show which sentence uses the word <u>before</u> as a **preposition**.

<u>Before</u> you go to bed, make sure you turn off the lights. ☐

Something must be done about this <u>before</u> it's too late! ☐

Eric made several phone calls <u>before</u> he left the office. ☐

Doing it this way is like putting the cart <u>before</u> the horse. ☐

1 mark

4. **Tick ONE BOX** to show which sentence is correctly punctuated.

Betty, much to her surprise has won, this month's competition. ☐

Betty, much to her surprise, has won this month's competition. ☐

Betty much to her surprise has won, this month's, competition. ☐

Betty much, to her surprise, has won this month's competition. ☐

1 mark

5. Complete the sentence below with an appropriate **co-ordinating conjunction**.

There's no use crying, _______________________ the opportunity is gone.

1 mark

6. **Tick ONE BOX** to show which sentence is a **question**.

Have everything collected by tomorrow afternoon ☐

What is left to collect from the shed is negligible ☐

Have you collected all your things from the hall ☐

Who collected all this rubbish is a mystery ☐

1 mark

7. **Tick ONE BOX** to show which sentence uses the word <u>clean</u> as a **verb**.

<u>Clean</u> your teeth properly after every meal. ☐

As her parents were visiting, Jackie gave the flat a good <u>clean</u>. ☐

Having a <u>clean</u> driving licence would help you get the job. ☐

Cinderella was amazed; the dirty clothes had been washed <u>clean</u>! ☐

1 mark

8. **Tick ONE BOX** to show which sentence uses **capital letters** correctly.

Yolanda travelled to a South Pacific island last year. ☐

The School Play is being performed next week. ☐

The winner of the nobel Peace Prize has been announced. ☐

The local Bakery will close this coming February. ☐

1 mark

9. Insert a **pair of commas** in the correct place in the sentence below.

War Horse a novel written by Michael Morpurgo and which is set

in World War I has been made into both a film and a play.

1 mark

10. Replace the underlined words in the sentences below with the correct **pronouns**.

"Look at those girls!" said the twins excitedly. "The raincoats <u>the girls</u> are wearing have

the same patterns as <u>the raincoats that belong to us</u>!"

1 mark

End of Test B! Now check your answers on p. 76!

42

1. **Tick ONE BOX** to show which sentence is punctuated correctly.

"Please be quiet" said Gina, "because the baby's asleep." ☐

"Please, be quiet," said Gina, "because the baby's asleep." ☐

"Please, be quiet," said Gina, "because the baby's asleep." ☐

"Please, be quiet," said Gina "because the baby's asleep". ☐ <u>1 mark</u>

2. **Tick ONE BOX** to show which of the following sentences is the most **informal**.

The coach told us not to be late for rugby practice. ☐

"Lateness to rugby practice will not be tolerated," said the coach. ☐

Make sure you arrive on time for rugby practice. ☐

"Be on time for rugby practice, guys!" said the coach. ☐ <u>1 mark</u>

3. **Tick ONE BOX** to show which underlined words form a **main clause**.

<u>When we woke up</u>, we discovered that it had been snowing. ☐

We might go to the seaside <u>if the weather is good tomorrow</u>. ☐

Millie grated the carrots and <u>Peter mashed the potatoes</u>. ☐

Our local MP, <u>whose name I can't remember</u>, is a woman. ☐ <u>1 mark</u>

4. Circle the two words that are **antonyms** in the following sentence.

After the frightening storm had eased, the turbulent waves of the

sea that had been so alarming gradually became more tranquil. <u>1 mark</u>

5. **Tick ONE BOX** in each row to show if the apostrophe is used for **possession** or **contraction**.

SENTENCE	Possession	Contraction
Jade hid Fred's glasses.		
Where's the remote control?		
Their dog's gone missing.		
Omar can't come to the party.		

<u>1 mark</u>

6. **Tick ONE BOX** to show which sentence contains a **relative clause**.

The clock that is on the mantelpiece is an antique. ☐

I didn't think the meal was that nice. ☐

If Carl gets that job, he'll be thrilled. ☐

I think I will buy that red dress over there. ☐

1 mark

7. **Tick ONE BOX** to show which sentence below is a **statement**.

You aren't driving too fast, are you ☐

He was asked to drive slowly ☐

Use your indicators when driving ☐

How well am I driving ☐

1 mark

8. Insert **capital letters** and **full stops** in the passage below so that it is punctuated correctly.

Hussein is the best striker in our team he didn't play last Saturday because he'd hurt his knee and we lost we're hoping he'll be better next weekend

1 mark

9. Insert a **pair of dashes** in the correct place in the following sentence.

Expensive designer clothes especially those which are made in Italy are regularly to be seen in magazines.

1 mark

10. Complete the sentences below by rewriting the verbs in boxes in the correct **tense**.

Iris and Sean had _________________________ their work by the time the bell rang.

to complete

The Great Pyramid of Giza's construction _________________________ over 4,000 years ago.

to begin

1 mark

End of Test C! Now check your answers on p. 76!

1. Write a **command** which could be the first step in the instructions for using a washing machine. Make sure you punctuate your answer correctly.

____

1 mark

2. In the sentence below, identify each of the clauses as either **main (M)** or **subordinate (S)**.

Saladin, the pure-bred Arabian, streaked ahead of the other horses, so he won the race easily.

1 mark

3. Circle the **conjunction** in each of the following sentences.

Steve runs because he wants to lose a few pounds.

Lionel, my friend, jogs every day, yet he is still unfit.

Once Marissa has been for a run, she does her stretches.

1 mark

4. **Tick TWO BOXES** to show which sentences contain a **determiner**.

Rick passed an interesting-looking bookshop.

Utterly exhausted, Vera sat down and sighed heavily.

The distant mountainous horizon was forbidding.

Tomorrow, I shall travel north.

1 mark

5. **Tick ONE BOX** to identify the **subject** of the following sentence.

Had he studied French at school, Malcolm would have been given the job.

school

French

job

Malcolm

1 mark

45

6. Insert **two commas** and a **semi-colon** in the correct places in the following sentence.

Helen my favourite cousin enjoyed watching the latest Star Wars film she'd been looking forward to it ever since they'd announced it was being made. <u>1 mark</u>

7. Circle the **possessive pronoun** in the following sentence.

The Browns are having lunch at a favourite restaurant of theirs: a small Italian bistro which has been mentioned in the local newspaper as it's won several awards. <u>1 mark</u>

8. Rewrite the verbs in the boxes below using the **past simple tense** to complete the sentence.

There ________________ a great deal of amusement at Charlie's expense yesterday when

| to be |

he ________________ over his shoelaces and ________________ into the paddling pool.

| to trip | | to fall |

<u>1 mark</u>

9. Insert a **pair of brackets** in the correct place in the following sentence.

Yesterday, I saw that dog steal two sandwiches one beef and one turkey as well as several sausages from the butcher's. <u>1 mark</u>

10. Identify the one **prefix** which can be added to all three of the following words to make their antonyms. Write your answer in the box.

democratic
embarrassed
returnable

<u>1 mark</u>

1. Circle the two words that are **synonyms** in the following passage.

Although the tiny elf was exceedingly timid, he was also perceptive.

Indeed, it was evident to all that it had been his observant remarks

that had prevented a disastrous war with the goblins.   1 mark

2. Circle the **relative pronoun** in the following sentence.

The teacher told me, "Your painting technique is as good as Harriet's

whose picture won my art prize last year."   1 mark

3. **Tick ONE BOX** to show which **punctuation mark** should be in the place indicated by the arrow.

The solution to the mystery, which, as indeed Sherlock Holmes himself finally admitted
was one that combined the bizarre with the mundane.   ↑

dash   ☐

hyphen   ☐

comma   ☐

semi-colon   ☐   1 mark

4. Use a word formed from the root word <u>delight</u> to complete each of the sentences below.

"What a _____________________ surprise to see you!" said Maria, beaming.

The children clapped their hands _____________________ at the news.   1 mark

5. Use an **adjective** formed from the word <u>suffice</u> to complete the following sentence.

I think there is _____________________ petrol in the tank for us to get home.   1 mark

6.   Insert **three hyphens** in the correct places in the following sentence.

Ashish has bought a state of the art computer which he will use for a lot of graphic design work along with editing videos and streaming music.

1 mark

7.   Rewrite the sentence below in the **active voice**. Make sure you punctuate your answer correctly.

Severe flooding has been caused in some places by the heavy rain.

____

1 mark

8.   Rewrite the verbs that are underlined in the following sentences so that they are in the **past progressive** form.

We <u>watched</u> the news on TV. The headlines <u>were</u> read out.

1 mark

9.   Complete the following sentence using a **noun phrase** containing at least three words. Make sure you punctuate your answer correctly.

Screaming loudly, ____

______________________________tried to escape from the fire-breathing dragon.

1 mark

10.   Circle the **adjective** in the following sentence.

"That's a likely story!" Bill harrumphed irritably in disbelief.

1 mark

End of Test E! Now check your answers on p. 77!

1. A large crack appeared in the ________________________________.
$\overline{1\ \text{mark}}$

2. Bella ________________________________ the right answer.
$\overline{1\ \text{mark}}$

3. The chocolate ________________________________ tasted delicious.
$\overline{1\ \text{mark}}$

4. First, ________________________________ the egg white from the yolk.
$\overline{1\ \text{mark}}$

5. The climbers made the ________________________________ successfully.
$\overline{1\ \text{mark}}$

6. The class watched the royal ________________________________.
$\overline{1\ \text{mark}}$

7. Ahmed is making ________________________________ progress.
$\overline{1\ \text{mark}}$

8. Phil is our ________________________________ monitor.
$\overline{1\ \text{mark}}$

9. Newton discovered the ________________________________ of gravity.
$\overline{1\ \text{mark}}$

10. The ________________________________ blew the candle out.
$\overline{1\ \text{mark}}$

End of Test! Now check your answers on p. 83!

1. Draw a line to connect each word to the correct **suffix** so that it makes an **adjective**.

Word

malice

thought

excite

Suffix

able

ious

ful

1 mark

2. Use the **conjunctions** from the box below to complete the following sentence. You may use each conjunction only once.

because   so   while

________________ I feel a lot healthier ________________ I am cycling to work now, I am

more tired in the evenings, ________________ I go to bed earlier.

1 mark

3. Draw a circle around the **subject** in the following sentence.

Last   Monday,   Boris   received   a   large   parcel   from   Jim,   his   cousin.

1 mark

4. Draw a line to connect each sentence to the correct **determiner**. You may use each determiner only once.

Sentence

"Do you want ___ apple juice or orange juice?"

"I don't like ___ kind; I prefer cranberry."

"That's funny; ___ sister is exactly the same."

Determiner

my

either

some

1 mark

5.   **Tick ONE BOX** to identify the option that must end with an **exclamation mark**.

What was the final score of the match ☐

That was a terrific match, wasn't it ☐

What an exciting match that was ☐

They said that it had been the most exciting match they'd ever seen ☐ _1 mark_

6.   **Tick ONE BOX** to show which sentence uses the **semi-colon** correctly.

This election will be a close one there is no clear winner; according to the polls. ☐

This election will be a close one; there is no clear winner according to the polls. ☐

This election will be; a close one there is no clear winner according to the polls. ☐

This election; will be a close one there is no clear winner according to the polls. ☐ _1 mark_

7.   Use an appropriate **adjective** to complete the following sentence.

The _______________________ artist's portraits were highly valued. _1 mark_

8.   **Tick ONE BOX** to show where the missing **inverted commas** should go in the sentence below.

☐ ☐ ☐ ☐

"Do you know when the submission deadline is? inquired Lydia. _1 mark_

9.   Put **one** dash in the correct place in the following sentence.

Gary stopped and stared in amazement he'd never seen such a huge cat! _1 mark_

10. **Tick ONE BOX** in each row to show whether the sentence is in the **present perfect** or the **past perfect**.

SENTENCE	Present Perfect	Past Perfect
Rick has asked for a bicycle for his birthday.		
He had wanted a moped.		
However, his parents have refused to buy him one.		

1 mark

End of Test A! Now check your answers on p. 77!

51

1. Replace the underlined words in the sentence below with the correct **pronouns**.

Jack and Jill are terribly irresponsible: <u>Jack and Jill</u> were meant to be here by 10 o'clock, but we are still waiting for <u>Jack and Jill</u>.

1 mark

2. **Tick ONE BOX** to show which sentence uses the **colon** correctly.

These shorts come in four colours: dark grey, light blue, black and neon pink. ☐

These shorts come in four: colours dark grey, light blue, black and neon pink. ☐

These shorts come in four colours: dark grey: light blue: black and neon pink. ☐

These shorts: come in four colours dark grey, light blue, black and neon pink. ☐

1 mark

3. **Tick ONE BOX** to identify the sentence that shows Carlos is **most likely** to visit us next month.

Carlos may visit us next month. ☐

Carlos could visit us next month. ☐

Carlos might visit us next month. ☐

Carlos shall visit us next month. ☐

1 mark

4. Insert a **comma** in the correct place in the following sentence.

Although it was old and rusty Roger loved his grandfather's toolbox.

1 mark

5. Draw a line to connect each sentence to its correct **function**. You may use each function only once.

Sentence	Function
How full of rubbish those bins are	statement
If they are full, empty the rubbish bins	question
Rubbish bins should be emptied regularly	exclamation
Those rubbish bins are still full, aren't they	command

1 mark

6. **Tick ONE BOX** to identify the sentence which is written in **Standard English**.

Mike thoughted about the problem long and hard. ☐

Horace and Omar been standing in the queue for two hours. ☐

Patty brought her laptop to work yesterday. ☐

Betsy drunk all her juice before she ate her sandwich. ☐

1 mark

7. Identify the punctuation marks on either side of the words <u>who had repeatedly lied</u> in the following sentence.

Jim — who had repeatedly lied — begged Nancy several times to forgive him.

____

1 mark

8. **Tick ONE BOX** to show which sentence uses **capital letters** correctly.

The national Health Service has recently celebrated its Seventieth Year. ☐

The national Health Service has recently celebrated its Seventieth year. ☐

The National Health Service has recently celebrated its seventieth year. ☐

The National Health service has recently celebrated its seventieth year. ☐

1 mark

9. In the passage below, circle the word that contains an **apostrophe** for **contraction**.

By the battle's end, it was clear the Russians had lost. No surprise, then, that the soldiers' morale was so low. As their opponents' cheers rang in their ears, each man thought it'd been a complete disaster.

1 mark

10. In the sentence below, circle all the **prepositions**.

Grace sighed contentedly as she sat beneath her favourite oak tree in her local park: it was a beautiful spring afternoon.

1 mark

End of Test B! Now check your answers on p. 77!

1. Using the boxes given, write the **expanded forms** of the underlined word or words in each of the following sentences.

Be gentle with those glasses; <u>they're</u> very fragile!

I <u>haven't</u> got any others so <u>you'll</u> have to be careful.

1 mark

2. Your teacher is helping you to correct the punctuation of the sentence in the following box. **Tick TWO BOXES** to show which pieces of advice you are given.

"Who goes there"? demanded, the sentry.

There should be speech marks after the word 'sentry', not the word 'there'. ☐

The question mark should be immediately after the word 'there'. ☐

There should be a question mark after the word 'sentry'. ☐

There should be a comma before the word 'demanded'. ☐

There shouldn't be a comma after the word 'demanded'. ☐

1 mark

3. **Tick ONE BOX** to show the meaning of the root <u>ped</u> in the word family below.

bi**ped**   **ped**al   centi**ped**e   **ped**estrian

walk ☐

many ☐

foot ☐

movement ☐

1 mark

4. **Tick ONE BOX** in each row to show if the use of the **comma** in the sentence is correct or incorrect.

SENTENCE	Correct	Incorrect
The saucepans, which were dirty had been left in the sink.		
The statue, a priceless Roman artefact, has been stolen.		
No matter how hard I begged, Diana refused to help me.		
Pete, Josh, Ravi, Ahmed, and Kyle all dislike yogurt.		

1 mark

5. Rearrange the words in the following statement to turn it into a **question**. Use the given words only. Make sure you punctuate your answer correctly.

Statement: All the sailors were wearing their uniforms.

Question: ____

1 mark

6. In the sentence below, circle the two words that show the **tense**.

For thirty years, Mr Thomas did precisely the same thing every morning — he made his wife a cup of tea.

1 mark

7. In each of the following sentences, underline the **main clause**.

Despite his many years of experience, Danny was not offered the job.

Andy sneezed violently when Fiona, his sister, spilt pepper everywhere.

Once they arrived, the police started to question the people who'd seen the accident.

1 mark

8. Circle the **conjunction** in each of the following sentences.

The customer won't leave until she is given a refund.

Rubin was pleased, for he'd managed to beat his own record.

1 mark

9. Tick **ONE BOX** in each row to show whether the clause in bold is a **main clause (M)** or a **subordinate clause (S)**.

SENTENCE	M	S
While they are good for you, you shouldn't eat too many tomatoes.		
I'm sitting in the back row and **Anna is sitting beside me**.		
Uncle Chris made a shocking announcement **as we were leaving**.		

1 mark

10. Circle the two **conjunctions** in the following sentence.

After Mark had walked all the way to the shops, he realised he'd left his wallet at home, so he had to go back for it.

1 mark

End of Test C! Now check your answers on p. 78!

1. Insert a **colon** in the correct place in the following sentence.

Rhoda squealed suddenly she'd just seen a mouse!

1 mark

2. Underline the word that completes the following sentence correctly.

Typically, sales of (stationery / stationary) increase at the beginning of term.

1 mark

3. Use the correct **possessive pronoun** to replace the underlined word or words in each of the following sentences.

These paperweights belong to <u>Josh</u>. These paperweights are ___________________.

The house is owned by <u>Mr and Mrs Green</u>. The house is ___________________.

That book belongs to <u>my sister and me</u>. It is ___________________.

1 mark

4. Explain the meaning of the word **synonym**.

____

____

1 mark

5. Write one word that is the **synonym** of the word <u>miserable</u>.

____

1 mark

6. Using **adverbs** derived from the adjectives in brackets, complete the following passage. One has been done for you.

Tina ______**spitefully**______ [spiteful] broke her younger brother's favourite toy. When

Ivan discovered this, he wept ___________________ [bitter]. Their mother, Gina, was

___________________ [understandable] furious with her daughter.

1 mark

7. How do the different **suffixes** change the meanings of the two following sentences?

Ali said that Polly felt quite <u>hopeful</u>.

This means that Polly ____

____

____

Ali said that Polly felt quite <u>hopeless</u>.

This means that Polly ____

____

____
1 mark

8. Rewrite the verbs in the boxes below using the **present progressive tense** to complete the sentences.

Neil ___________________ by the phone as he ___________________ anxiously

| sit | | wait |

for a call from his girlfriend.

Tod ___________________ about all the work he has to do.

| whinge |
1 mark

9. **Tick ONE BOX** to show which option completes the following sentence correctly.

" _________ been sleeping in my bed?" growled Papa Bear.

Whose ☐

Whom ☐

Who's ☐

Which ☐
1 mark

10. In the following sentence, underline the **relative clause**.

That house that is painted blue has just been sold to an Italian family.   1 mark

End of Test D! Now check your answers on p. 78!

1. Use the word <u>insult</u> as a **verb** in a sentence of your own. Do not change the word. Make sure you punctuate your sentence correctly.

____

1 mark

2. Use the word <u>insult</u> as a **noun** in a sentence of your own. Do not change the word. Make sure you punctuate your sentence correctly.

____

1 mark

3. **Tick ONE BOX** in each row to show if the sentence is written in the **active voice** or the **passive voice**.

SENTENCE	Active	Passive
Cotton has been grown in Egypt for centuries.		
It is famous for its long fibre which makes it softer and stronger.		
In the past, it has been called 'white gold'.		

1 mark

4. Rewrite the sentence below in the **passive voice**. Make sure you punctuate your answer correctly.

Millions of people are watching the World Cup.

____

1 mark

5. Circle each of the two **adjectives** in the sentence.

The poor ugly duckling cried softly to himself when his brothers and

sisters laughed cruelly at him.

1 mark

6. Put one **colon** in the correct place in the following sentence.

Ravi wants to become a botanist a person who studies plants.

1 mark

58

7. **Tick ONE BOX** to show how the underlined words in the sentence below are used.

<u>Later that day</u>, Jorge realised what he'd forgotten to do in the morning.

a subordinate clause ☐

a fronted adverbial ☐

a noun phrase ☐

a relative clause ☐

1 mark

8. **Tick ONE BOX** to select the verb that completes the sentence in the **subjunctive form**.

It is vital that the headmaster ________ made aware of this.

were ☐

is ☐

are ☐

be ☐

1 mark

9. **Tick ONE BOX** to identify the function of the underlined words in the following sentence.

"I can't believe you've lost <u>both pairs of sunglasses</u>!" exclaimed Wilma.

a subordinate clause ☐

a preposition phrase ☐

a noun phrase ☐

a relative clause ☐

1 mark

10. **Tick ONE BOX** to show which sentence uses the **present perfect** form.

Felicity admitted that she had eaten all the chocolate cake. ☐

Pirates were lying in wait for the admiral's treasure ship. ☐

Since she started her new job, Rachel has been much happier. ☐

After the announcement was made, everyone began to make phone calls. ☐

1 mark

End of Test E! Now check your answers on p. 78!

1. Teresa works for a travel ________________________________.

1 mark

2. The school ________________________________ sang beautifully.

1 mark

3. Heba must not ________________________________ her mobile again.

1 mark

4. The king's ________________________________ lasted twenty years.

1 mark

5. The ________________________________ blew his whistle.

1 mark

6. The tree's bark was ________________________________.

1 mark

7. Sherif's pencil has a soft ________________________________.

1 mark

8. Warm clothing is ________________________________ in winter.

1 mark

9. There was ________________________________ among the politicians.

1 mark

10. Demeter ________________________________ the loss of her daughter.

1 mark

End of Test! Now check your answers on p. 84!

1. **Tick ONE BOX** to show which sentence should end with a **question mark**.

He didn't know how much it cost ☐

Ask Paul how much it costs ☐

How much did it cost ☐

Tell me how expensive it was ☐

1 mark

2. **Tick ONE BOX** to show which **pair of verbs** completes the sentence correctly.

In the fifteenth century, Leonardo da Vinci's flying machine _____ considered _____ revolutionary; now, however, the aeroplane is commonplace.

was   being   ☐

was   to be   ☐

were   to be   ☐

is   being   ☐

1 mark

3. **Tick ONE BOX** to show which sentence is correctly punctuated.

Completely exhausted, the climber finally reached the summit. ☐

Completely exhausted the climber finally reached, the summit. ☐

Completely exhausted the climber finally, reached the summit. ☐

Completely, exhausted the climber finally reached the summit. ☐

1 mark

4. **Tick ONE BOX** to show which sentence is in the **past tense**.

London Zoo is a popular tourist attraction. ☐

It houses almost 1000 different species. ☐

It is situated in Regent's Park in Central London. ☐

The zoo was intended to be used for scientific study. ☐

1 mark

5. Circle one word in each underlined pair to complete the sentences below in **Standard English**.

When I **come / came** in, I saw her.

She **was / were** wearing black trousers.

1 mark

61

6. Draw a line to match each **prefix** to the correct word so that it makes a new word.

Prefix | Word

sub — hear

dis — cast

non — miss

fore — sense

mis — stance

1 mark

7. In the box, write the **contracted form** of the underlined words.

I have decided that I <u>shall not</u> go to the gym tomorrow.

1 mark

8. Tick ONE BOX to show which sentence should end with an **exclamation mark**.

She asked me whether I was leaving ☐

You won't leave tomorrow, will you ☐

How rude of them to tell me to leave ☐

She was asked to leave the next day ☐

1 mark

9. Tick ONE BOX to show which sentence uses an **apostrophe** correctly.

Two rowdy players' names were taken down by the referees. ☐

Two rowdy player's names were taken down by the referees. ☐

Two rowdy players names' were taken down by the referees. ☐

Two rowdy players names were taken down by the referee's. ☐

1 mark

10. Circle all the **pronouns** in the following sentence.

As Tom was hungry, he poured himself a glass of milk and made himself two large cheese sandwiches with chutney and tomatoes in them.

1 mark

End of Test A! Now check your answers on p. 78!

1. **Tick ONE BOX** to show what the word <u>these</u> refers to in the following passage.

Our local museum is famous for its collections of Roman jewellery, weapons and mosaics. Many of <u>these</u> portray scenes from everyday life.

scenes ☐

collections ☐

mosaics ☐

weapons ☐

1 mark

2. Complete the following sentence with an **adjective** formed from the verb <u>talk</u>.

Mrs Lewis, who is over eighty, is an extremely ______________________________

person who loves telling stories about her past.

1 mark

3. **Tick ONE BOX** to show which part of the sentence is a **relative clause**.

At the top of the steep hill stands the house which is said to be haunted.

☐ ☐ ☐ ☐

1 mark

4. **Tick ONE BOX** to show **how** the underlined words are used in the sentence.

Unless everyone hurries up and gets in the car right now, <u>we'll be late</u>!

as a preposition phrase ☐

as a main clause ☐

as a noun phrase ☐

as a relative clause ☐

1 mark

5. Name the **punctuation mark** used between the two main clauses in the sentence below.

We agreed that Marie's party, which was last Friday evening, was a complete success: there wasn't a single complaint from anyone, even Martha!

____

1 mark

6. **Tick ONE BOX** in each row to show how the **modal verb** affects the meaning of each sentence.

SENTENCE	Certainty	Possibility
If you don't put on something warm, you might catch a cold.		
As Kelly's car has broken down, she will be late.		
Surprisingly, crocodiles can move very quickly.		
We could have cauliflower cheese for supper tonight.		

1 mark

7. **Tick ONE BOX** in each row to show whether the clause in bold is a **main clause (M)** or a **subordinate clause (S)**.

SENTENCE	M	S
Ants, **which live in colonies**, are found almost everywhere.		
Amazingly, in England alone, **there are over a hundred different species**.		
Although they can be annoying, **ants do help the environment**.		

1 mark

8. Circle **ALL** the **conjunctions** in the following sentences.

Whenever Tina goes to visit her grandfather, she always bakes him a chocolate cake, which is his favourite dessert.

Last week, Tina thought she would try something different and made him a carrot cake.

Although her grandfather was not very enthusiastic initially, after he had tried the carrot cake, he decided he liked it too.

1 mark

9. Circle the two words in the following sentence that are **synonyms**.

The frail old man slowly hobbled up the path, his feeble movements arousing pity among the sympathetic bystanders.

1 mark

10. **Tick ALL** the sentences that contain a **preposition**.

They couldn't see what lay beyond the hill. ☐

We left the theatre after the play had ended. ☐

He hasn't visited us since September. ☐

A bicycle knocked her over. ☐

1 mark

End of Test B! Now check your answers on p. 79!

1. Use the word <u>permit</u> as a **noun** in a sentence of your own. Do not change the word. Make sure you punctuate your sentence correctly.

____

1 mark

2. Use the word <u>permit</u> as a **verb** in a sentence of your own. Do not change the word. Make sure you punctuate your sentence correctly.

____

1 mark

3. **Tick ONE BOX** to show the meaning of the root <u>manu</u> in the word family below.

manuscript   manual   manufacture

to write ☐

by oneself ☐

by hand ☐

to create ☐

1 mark

4. Draw a line to match each word to its correct **antonym**.

Word	**Antonym**
surrender	expose
conceal	direct
curtail	elongate
serpentine	resistance

1 mark

5. Rewrite the following sentence, adding a **subordinate clause**. Remember to punctuate your sentence correctly.

Sita was watching a snooker match.

____

1 mark

6. Label the boxes below with **V (verb)**, **S (subject)** and **O (object)** to show the parts of the sentence.

While <u>Karim</u> <u>was waiting</u> for the doctor, the nurse took <u>his temperature</u>.

1 mark

7. Circle all the words in the sentences below that should start with a **capital letter**.

alexander   the   great   was   tutored   by   aristotle,   the   famous   philosopher.

alexander   became   the   ruler   of   macedonia   when   his   father   died.

1 mark

8. **Tick ONE BOX** to show which sentence is written in the **active voice**.

There were many brave soldiers in the army. ☐

The library books were returned on time. ☐

An emergency meeting was held in the town hall. ☐

Three days ago, our neighbour's car was stolen. ☐

1 mark

9. **Tick ONE BOX** to show which sentence is punctuated correctly.

She might come to the party — you never know with her but, I think it's highly unlikely. ☐

She might come to the party, you never know with, her — but I think it's highly unlikely. ☐

She might come to the party — you never know with her but — I think it's highly unlikely. ☐

She might come to the party — you never know with her — but I think it's highly unlikely. ☐

1 mark

10. **Tick ONE BOX** to show the correct place for a **semi-colon** in the sentence below.

The dinosaur skeleton was a hit at the museum the other exhibits were not as popular.

1 mark

End of Test C! Now check your answers on p. 79!

1. **Tick ONE BOX** to show which sentence below uses the **present progressive**.

The deer were grazing in the glade. ☐

The rabbits have eaten all our carrots. ☐

The grasshoppers are making a terrible racket. ☐

We saw two robins building their nest in a plant pot. ☐

1 mark

2. **Tick ONE BOX** to show which sentence below is a **command**.

I want everyone to come to the meeting. ☐

Don't be late tomorrow morning. ☐

You need to be here at 10 o'clock sharp. ☐

Everyone should bring a notebook and a pencil. ☐

1 mark

3. Rewrite the following statement as **direct speech**. Remember to punctuate your answer correctly.

The zoo-keeper warned them not to give the monkeys nuts.

The zoo-keeper warned them, ____

____

1 mark

4. Insert a pair of **brackets** in the correct place in the following sentence.

All   of   the   men   who   had   fought   so   valiantly   received   medals   from

the   king.

1 mark

5. **Tick ONE BOX** in each row to show if the underlined word is an **adjective** or an **adverb**.

SENTENCE	Adjective	Adverb
We haven't been there <u>lately</u>.		
They were <u>hard</u> workers.		
I haven't seen him <u>before</u>.		
The man walked <u>very</u> slowly.		

1 mark

6. Complete the following sentence with an **adverb** formed from the adjective <u>responsible</u>.

Before they went out for the evening, Mr and Mrs Lee asked their children to behave

_______________________________________.

1 mark

7. **Tick ONE BOX** to show which sentence below uses the **hyphen** correctly.

Mrs Brown always attends the end-of-term-party at school. ☐

Mrs Brown always attends the end-of-term party at school. ☐

Mrs Brown always attends the end of-term-party at school. ☐

Mrs Brown always attends the-end-of-term party at school. ☐

1 mark

8. Rewrite the following sentence in the **passive voice**. Punctuate your sentence correctly.

A loud noise woke her in the middle of the night.

____

1 mark

9. **Tick ONE BOX** in each row to show whether the word <u>since</u> is being used as a **preposition** or as a **subordinating conjunction**.

SENTENCE	Preposition	Subordinating conjunction
He has not been seen <u>since</u> 10 o'clock last night.		
My scarf's been missing <u>since</u> the rugby match at the weekend.		
Sadly, our team hasn't won a match <u>since</u> we beat Arsenal last season.		

1 mark

10. Complete the following sentence so that it uses the **subjunctive form**.

I suggest that he _____________________________ harder to improve his technique. 1 mark

End of Test D! Now check your answers on p. 79!

1. Complete the following table by adding a **suffix** to each noun to make an **adjective**.

Noun	Adjective
hunger	
euphoria	
emotion	
rage	
shine	

1 mark

2. **Tick ONE BOX** in each row to show whether the word in bold is a **subordinating conjunction** or a **co-ordinating conjunction**.

SENTENCE	Subordinating conjunction	Co-ordinating conjunction
If you work hard, they say, you will succeed.		
She practises regularly, **whereas** he doesn't.		
Their team won, **for** they trained all year.		

1 mark

3. Circle all the **determiners** in the following sentence.

There isn't much salt left, so you must buy some tomorrow.

1 mark

4. Write a sentence that lists all the information given in the following box. Remember to punctuate your answer correctly.

> **Things you need to make a rabbit hutch**
>
> ply wood
>
> wire mesh
>
> hinges
>
> a bolt lock
>
> screws

____

____

____

1 mark

5. Underline the longest possible **noun phrase** in the following sentence.

James, my friend, is hoping that he will get a role in our school play.   1 mark

6. Underline the **verb form** in the **present perfect** in the following passage.

Jake had thought that living in the countryside would be boring. However, since his family moved to their new cottage, he has made many new friends and spends hours exploring his new surroundings.   1 mark

7. Complete the following sentence with a **possessive pronoun**.

Those books belong to them; they are _________________________.   1 mark

8. Circle the **adverb** in the following sentence.

After they had searched everywhere, they found their missing ball behind the garden shed.   1 mark

9. Insert a **colon** in the correct place in the following sentence.

Cats can be very lazy creatures sometimes, all they do is eat and sleep.   1 mark

10. **Tick ONE BOX** to show which **punctuation mark** should be in the place indicated by the arrow.

Leyton said, "There's no more milk" Jane had thought there was some left in the fridge.
↑

comma	☐
ellipsis	☐
full stop	☐
hyphen	☐

1 mark

End of Test E! Now check your answers on p. 79!

1. His opponent's __________________________ let Jeff score a goal.

1 mark

2. Our bodies use __________________________ to build muscles.

1 mark

3. Anna's house is __________________________ and well-furnished.

1 mark

4. Ben's father is a __________________________ advisor.

1 mark

5. Wanda __________________________ the deli on her way home.

1 mark

6. Wellington __________________________ a plan to beat Napoleon.

1 mark

7. Rose looked up the book in the __________________________.

1 mark

8. The __________________________ flew down the hill.

1 mark

9. Saul's handwriting is __________________________.

1 mark

10. The dog guarded his master's __________________________.

1 mark

End of Test! Now check your answers on p. 84!

Grammar & Punctuation Tests Marking Guidelines

Before using the Answers, please note the following:

Marks
- In all the Grammar and Punctuation Tests, each **correct answer** is worth **1 mark**.
- Half marks **may not be awarded**.

Multiple Answers
- When a question requires **more than one answer**, **ALL** the student's given **responses must be correct** for their answer to be regarded as right. For example, if the correct answers are the words *his* and *him*, the student must provide <u>both</u> correct words.
- When a question can be **correctly answered in more than one way**, this is noted in this section and an **example** of at least **one possible correct** answer is given.

Additional Marking Guidance
- Where necessary, additional marking guidance has been supplied in italics.

Answers to 'Tick Box' Questions
- Where the student must show their chosen answer by ticking at least one box, this section gives the correct answer(s), followed by which box(es) should be ticked: *1st box, 2nd box, 3rd box, etc.*
  - For sets of vertical boxes, the topmost box is the 1st box, and so on.
  - For sets of horizontal boxes, the leftmost box is the 1st box, and so on.

Answers

Group 1: Test A (pp. 6-7)

(1) Where are the plates kept *(4th box)*
(2) ...postponed <u>again;</u> this is...
(3) Sandy, my Aunt Mabel's parrot, is very bad-tempered. *(1st box)*
(4) to think again *(3rd box)*
(5) has locked *(2nd box)*
(6) was; were; were

(7) After 2011, conditions in the country appeared *(3rd box)*
(8) Kim discovered she'd run out of sugar, milk, butter, cheese and tea. *(2nd box)*
(9) conjunction *(3rd box)*
(10) ...green <u>umbrella: it</u> was... *(3rd box)*

Group 1: Test B (pp. 8-9)

(1) verbs *(4th box)*
(2) Lola was very confused — she couldn't understand where everyone had gone. *(1st box)*
(3) At the cinema, Charlie likes to sit in the <u>back</u> row. *(3rd box)*
(4) The twins (Annie and Molly) are playing a card game. *(2nd box)*
(5) *Answers will differ. Example:* after.

(6) What an awful accident *(3rd box)*
(7) The knight <u>left</u> the castle early the next day. *(2nd box)*
(8) I've never been inside the Houses of Parliament. *(4th box)*
(9) ...out<u>, despite the terrible weather,</u> to...
(10) Nora and Joyce → they; the cakes → them

(1) Vera exclaimed, "It took me hours to clean up that mess!" *(3rd box)*
(2) All residents must ensure the gate is locked at night. *(4th box)*
(3) The cowboy stopped what he was doing <u>when he heard the gunshot</u>. *(2nd box)*
(4) boring; engaging
(5) Let's have... → contraction; We've got... → contraction; ...the farmers'... → possession;
...Jeff's shoes... → possession
(6) The shirts which are in that drawer all need mending. *(1st box)*
(7) You can keep the book for two weeks *(2nd box)*
(8) ...his mother<u>.</u> He went...ingredients<u>.</u> <u>W</u>hen he...fruit salad<u>.</u>
(9) ...Nina<u>, her best friend,</u> have...
(10) to take → took; to have → has **OR** will have **OR** had

(1) *Answers will differ. Example:* First, wash the salad items.
(2) We put away our things → (M); after the bell rang → (S); we left the classroom → (M)
(3) Once; but; Whenever
(4) Polly waited for the bus. *(1st box)*; Mr Harris stared at his ruined suit. *(4th box)*
(5) Olivia *(2nd box)*
(6) ...<u>Arkadia,</u> there...the <u>Griffin — the</u> last...
(7) whose
(8) to have → had; to feel → felt; to eat → ate
(9) ...II <u>(the famous pharaoh)</u> used...
(10) dis- **OR** dis

(1) answer; respond **OR** to answer; to respond
(2) hers
(3) full stop *(4th box)*
(4) considerate **OR** inconsiderate; consideration
(5) argument
(6) ...terribly <u>far-fetched</u> until...the <u>world-famous</u> footballer...
(7) Reem gave Christopher an expensive present. **OR** Reem gave Christopher a present.
(8) works → is working; plans → is planning
(9) *Answers will differ. Example:* The wily hunter...
(10) carefully

(1) amuse → ing; weight → less; sphere → ical
(2) <u>If</u> they...cake <u>or</u>...dessert, <u>but</u> not...
(3) article **OR** an article
(4) Is there ___ milk left? → any; No. There is ___ juice, though. → some; Okay. I'll go to ___ shop later. → the
(5) Have you any idea why she dislikes broccoli *(3rd box)*
(6) You will need three things: a compass, a pen and a magnet. *(2nd box)*
(7) *Answers will differ. Example:* slowly.
(8) ...observed, Our *(2nd box)*; place. *(4th box)*
(9) ...<u>street,</u> Jonah...
(10) My brother is... → present progressive; He and his wife were... → past progressive; Now, they are... → present progressive

(1) Rachel → she; The lights → They
(2) In the middle of the jungle, the explorer stumbled across a well-worn path. *(2nd box)*
(3) Nancy will be angry. *(4th box)*
(4) ...<u>valuable;</u> that...
(5) Friends ought to be... → question; Friends are meant... → statement; If you are really... → command;

What an amazing... → exclamation
(6) That jockey has ridden horses since he was five. *(3rd box)*
(7) dashes **OR** a pair of dashes
(8) My least favourite novel by Charles Dickens is *Great Expectations*. *(1st box)*
(9) Bella's
(10) outside; of; on

(1) didn't → did not; he'd → he would; I'm → I am
(2) There should be a question mark after the word 'there', not a comma. *(3rd box)*; There should be inverted commas before the word 'yelled'. *(5th box)*
(3) self *(3rd box)*
(4) I don't like... → correct; Luis who always... → incorrect; Neither Tom, nor... → incorrect; Despite the extreme... → correct

(5) Is Carl more sensible than his brother?
(6) were; was
(7) ...to fight <u>even though he was badly wounded</u>; "<u>If you are tired</u>," advised...; <u>Wherever he went</u>, the man...
(8) for; Once
(9) ...which is kept in the cupboard... → (S); ...we decided not to wait. → (M); ...if Sherif wins the competition. → (S)
(10) and; but

(1) As soon as they had left <u>Greg,</u> Ian and Ahmed started to cough.
(2) As soon as they had <u>left, Greg,</u> Ian and Ahmed started to cough.
(3) theirs; hers; ours
(4) *Answers will differ. Example:* An antonym is a word that is opposite in meaning to another word.
(5) *Answers will differ. Example:* generous.

(6) ambitious; attentive
(7) *Answers will differ. Examples:* increased → made greater; decreased → made less.
(8) throw → threw; use → used; hop → hopped
(9) whose *(3rd box)*
(10) <u>which is hanging in my room</u>

(1) *Answers will differ. Example:* She asked me to <u>set</u> the table.
(2) *Answers will differ. Example:* As a child, I had a wooden train <u>set</u>.
(3) Jeff found a... → active; It had been... → passive; Jeff took it... → active
(4) Mr Simon took the pupils to the

assembly hall.
(5) badly; too
(6) ...<u>clear:</u> poverty.
(7) a noun phrase *(3rd box)*
(8) were *(4th box)*
(9) question *(2nd box)*
(10) Rob has been working hard and has improved as a result. *(1st box)*

Group 3: Test A (pp. 28-29)

(1) When is the train due to arrive *(4th box)*
(2) were   have *(2nd box)*
(3) Carefully picking it up, the knight inspected the crystal goblet. *(4th box)*
(4) She decided to become a teacher when she was 12. *(3rd box)*
(5) were; was
(6) dis → appoint; sub → merge; re → read; fore → ground; im → plausible
(7) would not → wouldn't
(8) He didn't know how much it cost, did he *(1st box)*
(9) The crowd's chants could be heard from a distance. *(2nd box)*
(10) She; herself; themselves

Group 3: Test B (pp. 30-31)

(1) dinosaurs *(1st box)*
(2) imaginative
(3) where he was born *(4th box)*
(4) as a noun phrase *(3rd box)*
(5) colon
(6) We might... → possibility; It could... → possibility; Bahaa can... → certainty; Vince may... → possibility
(7) he checked the time → M; which had been a present from his uncle → S; he'd been worried that he'd be late → M
(8) because; after; Although
(9) ill; healthy
(10) A small frog hopped onto the large lily pad. *(3rd box)*; The results will be announced towards midday. *(4th box)*

Group 3: Test C (pp. 32-33)

(1) *Answers will differ. Example:* I must <u>object</u> to that.
(2) *Answers will differ. Example:* The gnome saw a shiny <u>object</u> in the grass.
(3) heat *(2nd box)*
(4) protest → accept; release → capture; illuminate → darken; opaque → transparent
(5) *Answers will differ. Example:* The pirate, <u>whose name was Percy,</u> grinned at his captives.
(6) <u>Felicity</u> → S; <u>watered</u> → V; <u>the plants</u> → O
(7) abraham; lincoln; united; states; he; april
(8) The news had resulted in a great deal of celebration. *(4th box)*
(9) The goblins — long the enemies of the elves — joined forces with the wizard. *(3rd box)*
(10) ...devastation — everything... *(3rd box)*

Group 3: Test D (pp. 34-35)

(1) Rania was reading the newspaper when her phone rang. *(4th box)*
(2) Once you've finished using the hoover, put it back in the cupboard. *(2nd box)*
(3) He told her, <u>"I will look after the children."</u>
(4) Ava (<u>whose</u> maternal...of <u>Canada</u>) wants...
(5) ...the <u>wrong</u> room → adjective; ...worked <u>hard</u> all... → adverb; ...a <u>quick</u> lunch → adjective; ...looked <u>straight</u> at... → adverb
(6) happily
(7) A sixty-five-year-old woman has broken the world record. *(4th box)*
(8) *Answers will differ. Example:* A brick was hurled through the window.
(9) ...choice <u>before</u> them... → preposition <u>Before</u> you go... → subordinating conjunction; <u>Before</u> the autumn... → preposition
(10) *Answers will differ. Example:* find.

Group 3: Test E (pp. 36-37)

(1) *Some answers will differ. Examples:* hair → hairy; dot → dotted; plenty → plentiful; horizon → horizontal
(2) Although → subordinating conjunction; for → co-ordinating conjunction; and → co-ordinating conjunction
(3) The; that; two
(4) *Answers will differ. Example:* To make hot porridge, you will need the following things: oats, milk, yoghurt, honey and brown sugar.
(5) Martin's story about his holiday
(6) has been
(7) theirs
(8) often
(9) ...three colours: light...
(10) dash *(4th box)*

Group 4: Test A (pp. 39-40)

(1) How pretty she looked in that gown *(3rd box)*
(2) ...problem — work.
(3) Last Tuesday, at the theatre, we saw a Shakespeare play: *Hamlet. (2nd box)*
(4) twice a year *(4th box)*
(5) has organised *(2nd box)*
(6) doesn't; don't; don't
(7) As fast as possible, Raymond raced *(1st box)*
(8) I want to read a book, watch TV, listen to music and go swimming at the same time. *(4th box)*
(9) conjunction *(1st box)*
(10) ...doorbell rang; we all... *(2nd box)*

Group 4: Test B (pp. 41-42)

(1) verbs *(3rd box)*
(2) I like the idea of a hybrid: a car that uses both petrol and electricity. *(2nd box)*
(3) Doing it this way is like putting the cart before the horse. *(4th box)*
(4) Betty, much to her surprise, has won this month's competition. *(2nd box)*
(5) for
(6) Have you collected all your things from the hall *(3rd box)*
(7) Clean your teeth properly after every meal. *(1st box)*
(8) Yolanda travelled to a South Pacific island last year. *(1st box)*
(9) War Horse, a novel...War I, has been...
(10) the girls → they; the raincoats that belong to us → ours

Group 4: Test C (pp. 43-44)

(1) "Please, be quiet," said Gina, "because the baby's asleep." *(2nd box)*
(2) "Be on time for rugby practice, guys!" said the coach. *(4th box)*
(3) Millie grated the carrots and Peter mashed the potatoes. *(3rd box)*
(4) turbulent; tranquil
(5) Jade hid Fred's... → possession; Where's the remote... → contraction; Their dog's gone... → contraction; Omar can't come... → contraction
(6) The clock that is on the mantelpiece is an antique. *(1st box)*
(7) He was asked to drive slowly *(2nd box)*
(8) ...our team. He didn't play...we lost. We're hoping...next weekend.
(9) ...clothes — especially...Italy — are...
(10) to complete → completed; to begin → began **OR** had begun **OR** was begun

Group 4: Test D (pp. 45-46)

(1) *Answers will differ. Example:* To start with, switch on the washing machine.
(2) Saladin, the pure-bred Arabian, streaked ahead of the other horses → (M); he won the race easily → (M)
(3) because; yet; Once
(4) Rick passed an interesting-looking bookshop. *(1st box)*; The distant mountainous horizon was forbidding. *(3rd box)*
(5) Malcolm *(4th box)*
(6) <u>Helen,</u> my...<u>cousin,</u> enjoyed...<u>film;</u> she'd...
(7) theirs
(8) to be → was; to trip → tripped; to fall → fell
(9) ...sandwiches (<u>one</u> beef...<u>turkey)</u> as well...
(10) un- **OR** un

Group 4: Test E (pp. 47-48)

(1) perceptive; observant
(2) whose
(3) comma *(3rd box)*
(4) delightful; delightedly
(5) sufficient **OR** insufficient
(6) ...a <u>state-of-the-art</u> computer...
(7) *Answers will differ. Example:* The heavy rain has caused severe flooding.
(8) watched → were watching; were → were being
(9) *Answers will differ. Example:* Screaming loudly, <u>the cowardly knight</u> tried to escape...
(10) likely

Group 5: Test A (pp. 50-51)

(1) malice → ious; thought → ful; excite → able
(2) <u>While</u> I...healthier <u>because</u>...evenings, <u>so</u> I...
(3) Boris
(4) "Do you want ___ apple juice... → some; "I don't like ___ kind... → either; "That's funny; ___ sister... → my
(5) What an exciting match that was *(3rd box)*
(6) This election will be a close one; there is no clear winner according to the polls. *(2nd box)*
(7) *Answers will differ. Example:* talented.
(8) ...is? inquired... *(3rd box)*
(9) ...amazement — he'd...
(10) Rick has asked... → present perfect; He had wanted... → past perfect; ...parents have refused... → present perfect

Group 5: Test B (pp. 52-53)

(1) <u>Jack and Jill</u> were → they; for <u>Jack and Jill</u> → them
(2) These shorts come in four colours: dark grey, light blue, black and neon pink. *(1st box)*
(3) Carlos shall visit us next month. *(4th box)*
(4) ...<u>rusty,</u> Roger...
(5) How full of rubbish... → exclamation; If they are full... → command; Rubbish bins should... → statement; Those rubbish bins... → question
(6) Patty brought her laptop to work yesterday. *(3rd box)*
(7) dashes **OR** a pair of dashes
(8) The National Health Service has recently celebrated its seventieth year. *(3rd box)*
(9) it'd
(10) beneath; in

(1) they're → they are; haven't → have not; you'll → you will
(2) The question mark should be immediately after the word 'there'. *(2nd box)*; There shouldn't be a comma after the word 'demanded'. *(5th box)*
(3) foot *(3rd box)*
(4) The saucepans, which... → incorrect; The statue, a priceless... → correct; No matter how hard... → correct; Pete, Josh, Ravi,... → incorrect
(5) Were all the sailors wearing their uniforms?
(6) did; made
(7) ...experience, <u>Danny was not offered the job</u>; <u>Andy sneezed violently</u> when...; ...arrived, <u>the police started to question the people who'd seen the accident.</u>
(8) until; for
(9) While they are good for you... → (S); ...Anna is sitting beside me. → (M); ...as we were leaving. → (S)
(10) After; so

(1) ...squealed <u>suddenly:</u> she'd...
(2) stationery *(1st word)*
(3) his; theirs; ours
(4) *Answers will differ. Example:* A synonym is a word that has the same meaning as, or a similar meaning to, another word.
(5) *Answers will differ. Example:* depressed.
(6) bitterly; understandably
(7) *Answers will differ. Examples:* hopeful → had hope; hopeless → had no hope.
(8) sit → is sitting; wait → is waiting; whinge → is whingeing
(9) Who's *(3rd box)*
(10) <u>that is painted blue</u>

(1) *Answers will differ. Example:* I did not mean to <u>insult</u> you.
(2) *Answers will differ. Example:* We all gasped at the terrible <u>insult</u>.
(3) Cotton has been... → passive; It is famous... → active; In the past, it has been... → passive
(4) *Answers will differ. Example:* The World Cup is being watched.
(5) poor; ugly
(6) ...<u>botanist:</u> a person...
(7) a fronted adverbial *(2nd box)*
(8) be *(4th box)*
(9) a noun phrase *(3rd box)*
(10) Since she started her new job, Rachel has been much happier. *(3rd box)*

(1) How much did it cost *(3rd box)*
(2) was   to be *(2nd box)*
(3) Completely exhausted, the climber finally reached the summit. *(1st box)*
(4) The zoo was intended to be used for scientific study. *(4th box)*
(5) came; was
(6) sub → stance; dis → miss; non → sense; fore → cast; mis → hear
(7) shall not → shan't
(8) How rude of them to tell me to leave *(3rd box)*
(9) Two rowdy players' names were taken down by the referees. *(1st box)*
(10) he; himself; himself; them

(1) mosaics *(3rd box)*
(2) talkative
(3) which is said to be haunted *(4th box)*
(4) as a main clause *(2nd box)*
(5) colon **OR** a colon
(6) ...you might catch... → possibility; ...she will be... → certainty; ...crocodiles can... → certainty; We could have... → possibility

(7) which live in colonies → S; there are over a hundred different species → M; ants do help the environment → M
(8) Whenever; and; Although; after
(9) frail; feeble
(10) They couldn't see what lay beyond the hill. *(1st box)*; He hasn't visited us since September. *(3rd box)*

(1) *Answers will differ. Example:* My parking <u>permit</u> has expired.
(2) *Answers will differ. Example:* The teacher will not <u>permit</u> us to do that.
(3) by hand *(3rd box)*
(4) surrender → resistance; conceal → expose; curtail → elongate; serpentine → direct
(5) *Answers will differ. Example:* Sita<u>, who is very enthusiastic about sport,</u> was watching a snooker match.

(6) <u>Karim</u> → S; <u>was waiting</u> → V; <u>his temperature</u> → O
(7) alexander; great; aristotle; alexander; macedonia
(8) There were many brave soldiers in the army. *(1st box)*
(9) She might come to the party — you never know with her — but I think it's highly unlikely. *(4th box)*
(10) ...museum; the... *(3rd box)*

(1) The grasshoppers are making a terrible racket. *(3rd box)*
(2) Don't be late tomorrow morning. *(2nd box)*
(3) *Answers may differ. Example:* The zoo-keeper warned them, "<u>Do not give the monkeys nuts.</u>"
(4) ...men (<u>who</u>...<u>valiantly</u>) received...
(5) ...there <u>lately</u> → adverb; ...<u>hard</u> workers → adjective; ...him <u>before</u> → adverb; ...<u>very</u>

slowly → adverb
(6) responsibly
(7) Mrs Brown always attends the end-of-term party at school. *(2nd box)*
(8) *Answers will differ. Example:* She was woken by a loud noise.
(9) ...seen <u>since</u> 10 o'clock... → preposition; ...missing <u>since</u> the... → preposition; ...match <u>since</u> we... → subordinating conjunction
(10) *Answers will differ. Example:* practise.

(1) hunger → hungry; euphoria → euphoric; emotion → emotional; rage → raging; shine → shiny
(2) If → subordinating conjunction; whereas → subordinating conjunction; for → co-ordinating conjunction
(3) much; some
(4) *Answers will differ. Example:* To make a rabbit hutch, you will need the following

things: ply wood, wire mesh, hinges, a bolt lock and screws.
(5) <u>a role in our school play</u>
(6) has made
(7) theirs
(8) everywhere
(9) ...lazy <u>creatures:</u> sometimes, all...
(10) full stop *(3rd box)*

Administering the Spelling Tests

- The **Spelling Tests** in this book **need to be read out loud** to the student from **the transcripts** provided in the following pages.

- Each spelling test in this book should take around 10 minutes.

- Before administering each spelling test, read out the following instructions.

  * *Listen carefully to these instructions.*
  * *There are 10 sentences in your test paper. Each sentence has a word missing from it.*
  * *I will first read the missing word on its own. Then, I will read the whole sentence with the missing word in it. Finally, I will read the missing word again on its own.*
  * *I will do this each time for each sentence.*
  * *Listen carefully to the missing word and write it in the space provided in your test paper.*
  * *Make sure you spell the word correctly.*

- Answer any questions the student may have before proceeding with the test.

- In the Transcripts, there are entries such as the one below:

  *Spelling 1: The word is **delighted**.*
  *Sam was **delighted** with his present.*
  *The word is **delighted**.*

- These should be read out to the student in the following manner:

  * *Read out loud "Spelling number 1."*
  * *Read out loud "The word is delighted."*
  * *Read out loud "Sam was delighted with his present."*
  * *Read out loud "The word is delighted."*

- Leave a gap of at least 12 seconds between each spelling.
- At the end, read all 10 sentences out again in order from the beginning.
- Give the student time to change any of their answers if they wish.
- When the test is over, say "This is the end of the test."

Marking the Spelling Tests

- Each **correctly spelt word** is worth **1 mark**.
- Half marks **are not to be awarded**.
- If a word requires a **capital letter, an apostrophe**, or **a hyphen**, these punctuation marks **must be used correctly** by the student **for the mark to be awarded**.
- Spellings that have been written as **two distinct** or **incorrectly hyphenated** words **cannot be accepted**.

Group 1: Spelling Test (p. 16)

Spelling 1: The word is **stationary**.
The **stationary** car's motor was still running.
The word is **stationary**.

Spelling 2: The word is **infectious**.
Measles is a highly **infectious** disease.
The word is **infectious**.

Spelling 3: The word is **preferred**.
Ihab has always **preferred** tea to coffee.
The word is **preferred**.

Spelling 4: The word is **changeable**.
The weather will be **changeable** today.
The word is **changeable**.

Spelling 5: The word is **principal**.
Mr Peters is the **principal** of our college.
The word is **principal**.

Spelling 6: The word is **receipt**.
Francis put the **receipt** in his pocket.
The word is **receipt**.

Spelling 7: The word is **desert**.
The reckless explorer got lost in the **desert**.
The word is **desert**.

Spelling 8: The word is **height**.
The nurse measured Riya's **height**.
The word is **height**.

Spelling 9: The word is **guitar**.
Brian has started taking **guitar** lessons.
The word is **guitar**.

Spelling 10: The word is **tragedy**.
Hamlet is a famous **tragedy** by Shakespeare.
The word is **tragedy**.

Group 2: Spelling Test (p. 27)

Spelling 1: The word is **orchestra**.
The youth **orchestra** gave a concert yesterday.
The word is **orchestra**.

Spelling 2: The word is **sandwich**.
Marcus had a toasted cheese **sandwich** for lunch.
The word is **sandwich**.

Spelling 3: The word is **drought**.
The persistent lack of rain caused a **drought**.
The word is **drought**.

Spelling 4: The word is **solemn**.
The mayor's speech was incredibly **solemn**.
The word is **solemn**.

Spelling 5: The word is **thyme**.
Chef Pierre used **thyme** to flavour the soup.
The word is **thyme**.

Spelling 6: The word is **trough**.
The thirsty cow drank from the water **trough**.
The word is **trough**.

Spelling 7: The word is **scientific**.
The laboratory was full of **scientific** instruments.
The word is **scientific**.

Spelling 8: The word is **descent**.
Slowly, the plane began its gradual **descent**.
The word is **descent**.

Spelling 9: The word is **business**.
Mr Smith ran a profitable **business** for years.
The word is **business**.

Spelling 10: The word is **efficiency**.
The **efficiency** of that machine is truly amazing.
The word is **efficiency**.

Spelling 1: The word is **malicious**.
The **malicious** rumour was started by Joel.
The word is **malicious**.

Spelling 2: The word is **envelope**.
Helen addressed the small **envelope** carefully.
The word is **envelope**.

Spelling 3: The word is **doubtful**.
Kristin looked **doubtful**, but she didn't argue.
The word is **doubtful**.

Spelling 4: The word is **practice**.
Our netball **practice** is always at four o'clock.
The word is **practice**.

Spelling 5: The word is **precede**.
An adverb can sometimes **precede** a verb.
The word is **precede**.

Spelling 6: The word is **alliance**.
Britain made an uneasy **alliance** with France.
The word is **alliance**.

Spelling 7: The word is **responsibility**.
Feeding the cat was John's only **responsibility**.
The word is **responsibility**.

Spelling 8: The word is **substantial**.
Penny's knowledge of geography is **substantial**.
The word is **substantial**.

Spelling 9: The word is **bough**.
An owl was perched on the tree's topmost **bough**.
The word is **bough**.

Spelling 10: The word is **cymbals**.
Mike has always wanted to play the **cymbals**.
The word is **cymbals**.

Spelling 1: The word is **ceiling**.
A large crack appeared in the **ceiling**.
The word is **ceiling**.

Spelling 2: The word is **guessed**.
Bella **guessed** the right answer.
The word is **guessed**.

Spelling 3: The word is **dessert**.
The chocolate **dessert** tasted delicious.
The word is **dessert**.

Spelling 4: The word is **separate**.
First, **separate** the egg white from the yolk.
The word is **separate**.

Spelling 5: The word is **ascent**.
The climbers made the **ascent** successfully.
The word is **ascent**.

Spelling 6: The word is **procession**.
The class watched the royal **procession**.
The word is **procession**.

Spelling 7: The word is **noticeable**.
Ahmed is making **noticeable** progress.
The word is **noticeable**.

Spelling 8: The word is **stationery**.
Phil is our **stationery** monitor.
The word is **stationery**.

Spelling 9: The word is **principle**.
Newton discovered the **principle** of gravity.
The word is **principle**.

Spelling 10: The word is **draught**.
The **draught** blew the candle out.
The word is **draught**.

Spelling 1: The word is **agency.**
Teresa works for a travel **agency**.
The word is **agency.**

Spelling 2: The word is **choir.**
The school **choir** sang beautifully.
The word is **choir.**

Spelling 3: The word is **lose.**
Heba must not **lose** her mobile again.
The word is **lose.**

Spelling 4: The word is **reign.**
The king's **reign** lasted twenty years.
The word is **reign.**

Spelling 5: The word is **referee.**
The **referee** blew his whistle.
The word is **referee.**

Spelling 6: The word is **rough.**
The tree's bark was **rough**.
The word is **rough.**

Spelling 7: The word is **lead.**
Sherif's pencil has a soft **lead**.
The word is **lead.**

Spelling 8: The word is **essential.**
Warm clothing is **essential** in winter.
The word is **essential.**

Spelling 9: The word is **dissent.**
There was **dissent** among the politicians.
The word is **dissent.**

Spelling 10: The word is **mourned.**
Demeter **mourned** the loss of her daughter.
The word is **mourned.**

Spelling 1: The word is **hesitancy.**
His opponent's **hesitancy** let Jeff score a goal.
The word is **hesitancy.**

Spelling 2: The word is **protein.**
Our bodies use **protein** to build muscles.
The word is **protein.**

Spelling 3: The word is **spacious.**
Anna's house is **spacious** and well-furnished.
The word is **spacious.**

Spelling 4: The word is **financial.**
Ben's father is a **financial** advisor.
The word is **financial.**

Spelling 5: The word is **passed.**
Wanda **passed** the deli on her way home.
The word is **passed.**

Spelling 6: The word is **devised.**
Wellington **devised** a plan to beat Napoleon.
The word is **devised.**

Spelling 7: The word is **catalogue.**
Rose looked up the book in the **catalogue**.
The word is **catalogue.**

Spelling 8: The word is **sleigh.**
The **sleigh** flew down the hill.
The word is **sleigh.**

Spelling 9: The word is **illegible.**
Saul's handwriting is **illegible**.
The word is **illegible.**

Spelling 10: The word is **possessions.**
The dog guarded his master's **possessions**.
The word is **possessions.**